A Will of His Own

of related interest

All Cats Have Asperger Syndrome
Kathy Hoopmann
ISBN 978 1 84310 481 0

Freaks, Geeks and Asperger Syndrome
A User Guide to Adolescence
Luke Jackson
Foreword by Tony Attwood
ISBN 9781843100980

The Complete Guide to Asperger's Syndrome
Tony Attwood
ISBN 978 1 84310 495 7

Talking Teenagers
Information and Inspiration for Parents of Teenagers with Autism
or Asperger's Syndrome
Ann Boushéy
ISBN 978 1 84310 844 3

Building a Joyful Life with your Child who has Special Needs
Nancy J. Whiteman and Linda Roan-Yager
ISBN 978 1 84310 841 2

Parenting Across the Autism Spectrum
Unexpected Lessons We Have Learned
Maureen F. Morrell and Ann Palmer
ISBN 978 1 84310 807 8

Laughter and Tears
A Family's Journey to Understanding the Autism Spectrum
Ann Hewetson
ISBN 978 1 84310 331 8

A Will of His Own

Reflections on Parenting a Child with Autism

Revised Edition

Kelly Harland

Jessica Kingsley Publishers
London and Philadelphia

First published in 2002 by Woodbine House, Inc.

This edition published in 2007
by Jessica Kingsley Publishers
116 Pentonville Road
London N1 9JB, UK
and
400 Market Street, Suite 400
Philadelphia, PA 19106, USA

www.jkp.com

Library of Congress Cataloging in Publication Data

Harland, Kelly.
    A will of his own : reflections on parenting a child with autism / Kelly Harland ; foreword by Jane Asher. -- Rev. ed.
       p. cm.
    ISBN-13: 978-1-84310-869-6 (pbk. : alk. paper) 1. Autism in children. 2. Autistic chil-
dren--Care. 3. Autistic children--Family relationships. 4. Parenting. 5. Child rearing. I. Title.
    RJ506.A9H268 2007
    618.92'85882--dc22

                                                              2007013866

British Library Cataloguing in Publication Data
A CIP catalogue record for this book is available from the British Library

ISBN 978 1 84310 869 6

Printed and bound in the United States by
Thomson-Shore, Inc.

For
Pat Close
Patti Corcoran
RinaMarie Leon-Guerrero
and
Jennifer Annable

Contents

Foreword

I have been involved with the world of autism for over twenty-five years and, from having known almost nothing about this complex condition all that time ago, it has become a very important part of my life. I have been lucky enough to learn a great deal about the autistic spectrum, not only from those with autism themselves and their families, but also from some of the pioneers and experts in the field—from Lorna Wing to Simon Baron-Cohen. But I would be the first to admit—as indeed I know all of those interested in autism would too—that there is still a great deal left to discover and understand about autism, and almost every day I learn something a little more to expand my still frustratingly limited knowledge.

We hear often nowadays of the distress and difficulty that autism can bring to those affected, but Kelly Harland's wonderfully clear, unsentimental and yet moving account of her daily struggles with Will brings a whole new perspective to our understanding. Her descriptions of the continually changing hopes and aspirations that she and her husband have for him will have echoes for every parent, especially those of children affected by this complex, multi-faceted condition.

The preconceived ambitions and objectives for their children that all parents unwittingly hold from the first awareness of pregnancy, are trampled on and crushed in those first few moments of horrified shock after a diagnosis of autism. From imagining their little darlings as anything from prime minister to nuclear physicist to prima ballerina, their projections come crashing down to land in a dusty heap of pathetically small hopes for the future: that they will grow up able to speak; able to make some sense of the world around them; able to be free from fear and abuse. Kelly's touching description of her joy at the realization that she and Will are actually taking part in what might (just) be called a "conversation" is a perfect example of the way that achieving the tiniest of goals can become a gigantic triumph when the hurdles against reaching it have been so great.

The obsessions and fears of autism, will, of course, resonate with all parents: all of my three went through various crazes (my youngest son, from the age of one or so, became entranced by vacuum cleaners, and, on every visit to friends, had to be taken to the broom cupboard to see their particular model—and yes, for his second birthday, I, like Kelly, had to produce a cake to match the obsession), and we all know of times when our children have been scared of the simplest things: from the night-time dark to the picture of a dragon on a corn-flakes box. But, unlike for my children, for those on the autism spectrum and those who care for them, these obsessions and irrational fears can be life-long and all-consuming, and Kelly's evocative descriptions of the effects this can have on everyday life make it easy to see just how relentless, distressing and exhausting this can be.

In spite of learning from the experts over the years, I've learned just as much about the subtleties of autism by reading accounts written either by those with the condition themselves, or by those close to them, and this clear-sighted description of Will's world and how it impinges on those around him is no exception. To be able to put ourselves in his shoes for a while not only helps us to understand something of the autistic spectrum, but also something of ourselves, and the weird way of looking at life that we consider "normal". A slight shift in our perceptions and we are there alongside him: haven't we all, at one time or another, been frightened by a sudden noise, whether school bell or ambulance siren? And haven't there been moments when the best of us would have loved to have thrown ourselves onto the ground in rage and panic at the cruelty and terror of human existence? Why does it seem perfectly natural to us to dream of and plan, at a young age, our educational path, but strange—even comic—to put equal effort into choosing which cookie or sandwich we'll have for lunch once we're at college? Reading the following pages makes you consider just how arbitrarily we set the rules and limits to what we consider acceptable behaviour.

But, above all, it is the love for Will—for what he *is*, not for what he might have been—that shines through this book, and we get to know him as a fascinating, intriguing and unequivocally worthwhile human being. Those with autism may have a very different way of looking at the world from the rest of us, but if we can just step back occasionally and see life through the eyes of those like him, we might learn, not only something about their problems and what we can do to help, but also about ourselves.

Jane Asher
President, National Autistic Society

Preface: A New "Will"

My son Will was eleven years old when the first edition of *A Will of His Own* was published, but for a long time before the book was released I found myself facing a moral dilemma. Naturally I worried over how Will might feel when the story of his life hit the stands—a story written, no less, by his mother. I knew he wouldn't really comprehend what it meant to have his private world exposed in print, but what if, in his own way, perhaps somewhere down the line, he did end up feeling as though he'd been betrayed? For a while I considered turning the deal down. When at last I decided that I would allow our precious, personal moments to be revealed to the reading public, I sat with Will and tried to explain to him that one day there would be a book on our bookstore shelf with his name on it, and that his parents thought it would be a great thing. I prayed he would understand, and went forward with my little project of love.

I needn't have worried for one moment. *A Will of His Own* is Will's favorite book, and he has read it from cover to cover at least fifty times.

This was the biggest and most surprising reward I received from the writing of *Will*. But there have been many others. Parents and educators have written to me from all over the world, telling me how grateful they are for the uplifting tales of a child who in so many ways is just like the children they know. At book signings I meet these readers in person, and realize that my son's gift has touched them in some remarkable way I could never have imagined.

And so in this new, revised edition of his story, I provide a tiny glimpse of William as he moves through his teenage years (in the last section, entitled "Willpower"). As a freshman in high school he happens to be flying a grand flag these days, living life and loving it. He's a member of the school jazz choir (where he is assisted mightily by his teachers and peers and has even been able to pull off a performance in front of an audience of hundreds). At home and at school he swims and bowls and practices yoga and rides his bike for miles. At least once a week he can still be found cruising Puget Sound with his dad on one of Seattle's wonderful ferryboats. His limitations, of course, are often a source of frustration —he struggles, trying to adapt to things that other people think of as easy. But as has always been the case, Will is a brave explorer who shines a bright light on every path before him. And he's surrounded by people—his parents, his teachers, his neighbors, his therapists, and even a number of his fellow high school students—who genuinely view him as an individual with something incredibly important to contribute to the world.

The irony of Will's autism is that it has opened up his life and mine to people we love and cherish; a dictionary definition of the term reads: "a disturbance in development where the formation of relationships cannot be fully established," and I think we've blown that one out of the water. In the original introduction to these essays I thanked many of Will's shining supporters, and now there are more. My deepest gratitude goes to Will's teachers, Dr. Candi Styer, Susanna Cole, and Colleen Derry, all three of whom gave so much to bring Will to his present place in school; to friends and educators Paula Donaldson, Cindy Nitz, Connie Gold, Kathryn Moogk, Carol Davis, Devin Gurley, Nancy Gruber, Carolyn Kelley, Jay Sasnett, Jo Ellen Hathaway, and Scott Brown; to Jen and everyone in Room 209A; and to my friends Sue Loppnow, Betsy Fay, Craig Morley, Jane Peck, Libby Torrance, Betsy and Morgan Wood, Christine Bagley and Patti Vincent, Rachel Paul, Barbara Benson, and Terry and Vickie Lauber, without whom life wouldn't be the same for my son. Thanks to all of our neighbors in the magical neighborhood —Margaret, Chris and Mark, Mary the Gardener, Deborah, Betsy and Nancy and Ann, the

Skoulases, and Arlene. Special thanks to Dr. John Whitehead, Will's brilliant psychologist and fun friend.

Thanks to Jane Asher for her great generosity and open heart, and to Helen Ibbotson and everyone at Jessica Kingsley Publishers.

And thanks most of all to my husband Chuck, who teaches our son about jokes and fun and adventure and music and self-discipline and friendship.

I began writing down my feelings about Will the day after he was diagnosed, and the inspiration came as much from pain and confusion as from his miraculous smile—it was a mixture of everything about my bouncing little two-year-old. Now years later—years that came and went in a flash, it seems—the words still pour forth onto my journal page, in a swirl of emotions that reflect the love and the hard parts and the triumph of walking side by side with this tall young man. Little did I dream that *A Will of His Own* would be more than a collection of anecdotes describing my wondrous child. It would be the whole story of my heart.

Kelly Harland
August 2007

A Different Song

Moonlight

This is where we are now.

It's an early September evening and Will and I are sitting on a wooden bench beneath a crescent moon. The sky is black, the air is crisp and cool with the onset of autumn, and high up in the dark the bright moon, hung at an angle, burns silver. We rest with our arms touching before a big fountain, the one that seemed such an unusual structure when it was first unveiled in the center of our upscale neighborhood shopping center a couple of years ago. It was designed to stand as an oasis amidst the buzzing palatial stores and quaint cafes that surround it, and now here it looms, a mini-Stonehenge-with-waterfalls, lit up like an attraction in the twilight. Will and I have learned to appreciate it, because the kids can actually play in it in summer, and on a night like tonight it soothes—it sings, as water spurts abundantly from the top of the big stones and splashes into the shining pool at their base.

Now the merchants are getting ready to lock their doors: we have already spent an hour or so inside the shops, not shopping, never shopping, but running all around as we always do, mother chasing boy, boy bumping into other boys who are picking out pencils in the school supplies section of the drugstore, boys chattering away about which color notebook to buy, on this eve of the week before my boy's third grade life begins. William simply cannot stand still in a school supplies aisle, or in any other section of any place of business. He bounces off the walls, he "sharks" as his occupational therapist calls it—runs the inside perimeter of the building, moving round and round and round at rapid speed. There is too much stuff in a store, too much for his brain to handle, so the aisles are enough—the aisles and the doors and the exit signs are what he sees and knows, the things that guide him through the chaos.

That race through stores, which began when Will was two (he is now ten) has become just a regular part of our lives, like a stroll in the park. So our dip into the drugstore lasts a total of three or four minutes, and the same for all the other stores in the village of shops. Then finally, here on the bench by the shimmering fountain, the chase is over and the little shark relaxes. We are in the open air, in the calm night, and there is nothing to stimulate but cascading water and its burbling melody. We are alone in the moonlight.

The conversation, led by him, goes like this:

"Elementary school has fourth grade and fifth grade left to go." His green eyes stare up at Stonehenge, reflecting silver light, flashing with thoughts.

"Yes," I say.

"After that, we don't know what middle school I'm going to choose."

"Right." He once drew a chart on his chalkboard of all the grades up through four years of college. Then he added: "Job—2 years."

"It could be Hamilton, or Eckstein." Will knows every last school building in the Seattle district. He's made his father and me drive past each one of them a hundred times. We've traipsed them on foot during off-hours and we know every corner and cranny. It is the layout of each school campus that pulls him—the halls, the boys' and girls' bathrooms. Little variations on a design that is, when set apart from bustling hollering crowds of students, so beautifully predictable.

"Could be." I'm really listening now, after doing our store-run on automatic pilot.

"Could be," Will echoes. My heart is brought up short. If there happened to be anyone passing by, this little boy's manner of speaking would sound odd. It comes out in a funny singsong, so baby-like for a child his size. And the mother's voice in response might sound casual, like a normal mom talking to her kid. But in true matter of fact, the kid is at his shining, unprecedented best and Mom is holding her breath. I am, as my soul starts to stir, trying to contain myself. This is a conversation. This is something that has been an incredible uphill battle for Will—something that we work hard, every day, to achieve. For years we've paid professionals to assist us with this. We've written stories about it to try to get it going. And now here it is, rolling along spectacularly, without struggle, the words sailing happily up into the luxuriant night air.

"After high school comes college." This is a new one on me. "Yes, college." I say. "Maybe," I add quickly.

"I'll go to the University of Washington. I'll have my lunch in the Student Union building. I'll have a cookie, a muffin, or a scone."

Now I feel the need to interject and not for reasons of nutrition. "People have to pay a lot of money to go there, you know, Will. Lots of people are trying to get in. We'll see." Why can't I just let him dream on, a child's dream? It's because I know. He gets these things in his mind and he is like no child or human I have ever seen. The thought forms in concrete and can't be moved. Once built, it stays and stays—till he graduates from high school and he's standing there confronting me as if no time had ever lapsed between this moment and the future. He'll be asking me then about the UW, I'm sure of it. But now the fall night crackles and he goes on—disregarding my warning, and to my utter amazement.

"After that I'll get a job. I'll live in an apartment down by the waterfront. I'll work at the Seattle Trade Center. I'll ride my bike."

Excellent! My concerns over how I'll create a private classroom at the UW vanish. I'm delighted with this design for a career track. I'm especially pleased that there is no car on it.

"I think there's a bike rack at the Trade Center," he says. Yes, as a matter of fact, there probably is. "I'll have an office…and a computer…and a view of the railroad tracks!" Certainly. Now the scent of some faraway harvest-night bonfire rides past me on the breeze and I am caught up. I snuggle into my sweater. This exchange is a miracle. I'm hearing about a dream—a dream!—from a boy whose way of thinking is so narrow and delayed it doesn't seem possible that a dream would be allowed in. And I'm imagining: the Trade Center. Can't one rent office space there? Couldn't I set something up?

"Maybe you'll even have an office door with your name on it!"

He scoots to the edge of the bench. "I'll have a sign that says: 'Will!'"

Everything in the shopping center is turned off, but the water in the fountain is still at play, tumbling and splashing in the spotlight, echoing Will's cry. So many nights I have lain awake as tears-mixed-with-prayers dampened my pillow. I've put in a lot of time in the dark, feeling heavy and helpless and terrified for a future I can't predict. But all of a sudden the future has revealed itself from the other side, and it's being held up before my eyes like an Olympic torch. Whatever has led us to this—years of speech therapy, hours upon hours of my own input based on instinct and a few educated guesses, his father's incredible talent for showing him a way to walk through this world—William can see his dream, and it looks good. In fact, it looks perfect. And he's telling me all about it.

The Shock of the New

We'd had a few weeks without a problem. I was beginning to take for granted the fact that we could move through a morning, an afternoon, perhaps even a whole day without a flip-out or a freak-out. Sometimes, in my indefatigable optimism, I get to a place where I really believe the whole nightmare is over—the nightmare that consists of watching the littlest thing suddenly send my child into tears and frantic helplessness. I actually start to relax, like someone whose sailboat is floating peacefully after being buffeted around by a storm. But something eventually comes up again, out of the blue, in a flash, an electrifying bolt.

This time it was those little sticks that divide up the groceries on the supermarket conveyor belt. I don't think the regular population notices them much—I don't even know what they're officially called. You pick them up, you set them between your purchases and the next guy's, you don't think twice about them. You've probably never noticed that they usually have the store logo on them. I know that I had never even looked at how many are grouped together beside the cash register until that day.

Will had never noticed the dividers before either, but on this day he did, and since he was seeing them for the first time, they threw him for a loop. They changed what was happening in his predictable check-out routine—push cart through, ring up purchases, pay money, go out to car. Something was different, and it surprised him.

I try to explain to people what "different" and "surprise" can do to our family, but I don't think it can be explained. Because when the moment strikes, when the fear comes over Will's face, when he throws the sticks and takes off and you run after him with the startled faces of shoppers in your mental rear-view mirror, when he gets in the car and bursts into hysterical tears and you put your hand over his heart and it's running at 150 beats a minute—well, life takes on a bizarre quality. Did a two-ton monster breathing flames pop up next to the grocery clerk? If only it were true—if it could be something that easy, something a shield and a spear could fix. No, to save the day in these situations—when your child is hyperventilating and turning ashen because he glimpsed a grocery store divider stick—you must wear a more ingenious kind of armor.

This happened on a perfectly glorious Seattle day, when we had been driving around in the sun, crossing our favorite city bridges and stopping off at parks and little bakeries and feeling like nothing could stop us. Then the day was ruined. Sometimes a bridge ruins the day—by sounding a clanging bell, stopping traffic and opening up for a boat to go through (this can be really bad). Sometimes the park ruins it—by sporting a section of new grass that is cordoned off by yellow tape. Sometimes the bakery is the culprit—normally they're open but today there is a "Closed" sign in the window. "Open" and "Closed" signs can affect Will's mood in the most significant way.

And though I've toughened, I mostly ride around on a roller coaster when it comes to these things. I panic, I groan, if I happen to be out on my own and I see a banner proclaiming "Going Out of Business" on one of Will's favorite stores. (A shop gets added to our "Favorites" list by virtue of the design of the sign over its door, or because of the doors themselves or the layout of the aisles—never because of the merchandise contained inside.) I know I must start working on a plan to break the news to William, who will be—well, devastated would not be too strong a word. He'll be crushed, and it will take him awhile, maybe weeks, to get over a loss that isn't at all sentimental. His feelings are based on something I can't fathom, the simple fact that something that was there, and that was there over and over again, is not there anymore.

His father and I have formed a little swat team. We will read a brief mention in our local newspaper of a corporate takeover—the "Pay-Rite" chain, it announces, will soon be sold and renamed "Buy More"—and to us the tiny headline stands out like a blaring billboard. Grateful for advance warning, the team immediately responds. When will we begin prepping our charge? How bad will it be? Chain store closures put us on the alert in the worst way. The store and its sign are the familiar, comforting landmarks that help our child find his way in the world. He lives for repetition, for sameness—it is a need that is built into him. My husband, Charles, and I know painfully well what is going to happen to all three of us when suddenly one day, in places all across the city, that big sign comes down.

Of the many things that affect our daily life—guiding our child through school, pressing him toward socialization, trying to expand his five-item food menu, finding ways to help him color a picture or glue pipe cleaners to construction paper when sensory overload and motor skill problems cause him to shy away from any kind of art work—it's our role as human buffers in the face of life's little changes that is the most difficult job Charles and I face, and the one that demands the most of us in terms of cleverness and cunning. There are tools. Early in Will's life we learned how to draw "social stories," little cartoon strips with stick figure boys doing the stuff every kid does, but mapped out in a straightforward way to explain the how and why. Since he locks onto a simple visual image, the cartoon strips can work like a charm. We've used these maps to assist us with everything from "How to Say Hello" to potty training. So now, if we are going to change something in a room in our house—let's say we are going to move in a new couch or are planning, believe it or not, to change a light fixture—we use them to stem the tide. It will take weeks of preparation to get him ready.

Here's how it begins. Day One: Will, I think I'm going to get a new comforter for my bed. Day Four: Will, I've found the comforter and it's coming sometime in May! In just a few weeks! Day Eight: We can't wait for our new bedding, can we? It will have blue flowers on it (by now I've purchased the fluffy intruder and it sits in the closet awaiting its debut). At last I whip out paper and pen. I draw an eight-panel story about Will discovering the new bed. "Something new is coming to my mom's bedroom," reads the caption underneath the first box, and the little stick figure Will has a question mark over his head. In the last box the stick kid jumps for joy. "It's okay!" reads the caption. "I'm getting used to changes! I like the new bed!" We read this every day for about two weeks straight.

It's a hit-and-miss operation. When we brought in a new sofa, everything worked great. But on the Day of the Comforter, Will threw a fit. He carried it out the back door and down our alley to a neighbor's recycling box hundreds of feet away. I retrieved it and gave it to one of my girlfriends.

Why does it happen? And why do things sometimes enter Will's life without a trace of shock or upset, allowing us a taste of what it would be like for Will to be "normal"? The autism that invades Will's entire person, that forces him to require concrete structure and repeating patterns in order to make sense of anything, can leave him in an extraordinarily vulnerable position if that structure is missing. Because of this, Will must feel threatened by many things, a lot of the time. His dad and I try to divide his scares into three categories: the small ones that dissipate in a minute or two; the ones that truly are traumatic; and the ones he uses to manipulate his parents, for yes, this bright little boy knows how quickly we run to his rescue when a moment from one of the first two categories arrives, and we are always trying to balance ourselves along that fine line.

Charles and I are constantly on the alert for signals, the way I imagine parents whose kids are allergic to certain foods do autopilot scans of snack tables at birthday parties. Often, like two soldier buddies in a trench, we anticipate the enemy and pull off a maneuver just in time. (Private Mom is preserved forever on one video, rushing to comfort Will because I know his party guests are about to sing "Happy Birthday," and I didn't forewarn him it was coming, and he is going to fall apart.) We do not do battle alone. Therapists have been on the case, and doctors, and anti-anxiety medication is now playing a role when all else fails. There is a lot of work, since this stuff comes up in its moderate form every day, and, as a straight-out-of-left-field electroshock, just about once a week.

The grocery store incident definitely rated as one of the electroshocks. In its aftermath, Will and I pulled ourselves together by talking about the divider sticks a lot, talking about why they upset him, and discussing why they are there and why we must get used to them. And now, when I go to the supermarket with him, I simply set my groceries on the conveyer belt far apart from the next guy's.

When I am in a toy store with Will and he never, never can allow me to buy him a toy—because to remove the item from the shelf (a change) would cause him distress—I have learned to firmly take hold of myself. Toys aren't everything, I force myself to think. I try not to hear the other little voices in the store pleading with their parents to buy them this and that. I try not to think about the fact that if I could, I would buy him the priciest toy in the store—I would buy him all the toys, if only he would let me. As Private Mom, of course, I go back to the store alone, pick out something surefire, and make a cartoon strip for it.

"I like things to be the same," Will often remarks proudly. It is his identity, and I am so grateful that he can express his feelings about himself. But it is the part of his identity that I want to see, and that I must believe I will see, change. The part that, when he tenses, when he runs, when he cries out in terror, I want to change into something utterly, drastically different.

Ferryboats

Along the Seattle wharf the noon sun lavishes gold light on brilliant blue water. Will and I are giggling and jogging all the way to the ferry dock, where the boats, white and proud with black-and-green trim, sit high overlooking the stairways and walkways of the busy terminal. As we hurry past the waterfront, the stately vessels get bigger, bigger. It is so exciting. All day long Will has been saying, "I'm finally hooked on ferryboats!"

Here is what he means: prior to this May day, in his young life, he has been hooked on escalators (mainly), elevators (a lot), exit signs, and the hand-dryers in public bathrooms. And as his little legs ran and danced toward and around and up and down these modern-day appliances, his parents followed. We had no other choice, it seemed. For William, a trip to the park to visit a four-dryer men's room seemed as fabulous as a visit to Disney World would seem to most other kids. We tried to talk him out of these obsessions, of course, and behavioral and occupational therapists worked to try to influence him in the same way, but no breakthrough came. So we gave our son his joy. We rode up and down a hundred escalators, and went to the aquarium so he could race past green sea life on his way to the green exit signs. We stood patiently as he pressed the magic button on automatic hand dryers from one end of the city to another. He'd wake up on a Saturday and crow, "Mama and Papa are going to take me to see blowers today!" Mama and Papa steeled themselves and looked around for a paperback novel to help them make it through the next "Blower Tour."

Friends say, "What patience!" A mother said to me, "What surrender!" It is true, I have surrendered, his father and I both have surrendered, our time, our hearts, our lives, our mental health. We've helped Will work hard in school, we've read to him, we've intervened at every opportunity to try to show him the treasures of life that do not necessarily go on and off, up and down. We would have taken him anywhere to get his mind off his fixations. But when it came time to play, well, we figured out the score—it was off to a skyscraper with forty-two floors.

But now we've made it to the ferry dock. We stand together staring up at our new obsession and I'm thinking that this—well, this could actually pass for normal. My boy loves boats! We can be here in the open air, in the sunshine. We can sniff the breeze of Puget Sound and, humbled by the size of the queenly ships, look up and study their uniform design. And naturally I know that's part of the attraction—they all look the same. I also know that they go back and forth, back and forth. But who cares? There is so much to ferry life, so many variations on the theme. Already today we have lingered at the entrance to the terminal where there hangs a series of sepia-toned photographs from the archives of Washington State. It tells the story of the early ferryboats. William stood still—stood still!—to study the prints. We are so beautifully far from being stuck in a whistling steel box, staring at numbers on a lighted panel!

Then comes the sound of the horn. "It's the Wenatchee!" cries Will, right on the money as he sees his boat slowly pulling out of the dock in all its glory, smokestack puffing. "And over there is the Hyak!" At home he will spend hours pretending he is a ferry (sometimes the captain and sometimes the boat) on its run, on all the routes from Seattle to the San Juan Islands. He recites the safety announcement again and again: "Smoking is only allowed on the upper deck—smoking is not allowed in the passenger cabin." He likes to cast me as the ticket taker. He builds models of each ferry out of Legos. He draws overhead maps of the boats. He keeps a collection of Northwest postcards depicting each one. He likes to say, "Mama, which one is your favorite?" I choose a favorite. I do not tell him that they all look the same to me.

Then, of course, the best part of all. We can ride them! We can take trips! My kid is beginning to understand that a reward may be waiting at the end. A park, a little street of tourist shops. He can find something of interest in these things, as long as he knows he'll be riding the boat. His grandmother's house is across the water. For a boy who is reluctant to try anything new, this magic fleet of carriers can help to widen his world.

The adventures do not come without a hitch. Once Will was scared out of his wits by a loud boat horn, so he now insists on wearing protective headphones on every trip. He can be ambushed by an excruciating anxiety attack if things aren't "the same"—if a particular boat on a particular run has been changed, or if the announcement that comes over the loudspeaker is different. (I try to explain to him that there are miscellaneous guys and gals improvising up there on the microphone, even though sometimes during one of his attacks I wish I'd gone up to the pilot house with a script.) Going on the boats is not like watching them move in and out of their places from afar. It is entering the real-life world of travel where anything can happen—a sometimes nerve-wracked, love-hate experience that confounds the whole family. But we have determined that it is somehow worth whatever we have to go through.

Last summer, the first summer of the ferryboat, we went to a city park to play in a big local wading pool, crowded with kids. Before I knew it, Will had splashed his way out to the middle of the pond, where I could barely see him but could hear him chanting, oblivious to everyone and everything: "Now arriving, San Juan Island!" He was thrilled to have real water for his game, and I relaxed on the bank, knowing that this would keep him occupied for awhile. But trouble arrived in the form of a lifeguard's whistle. A buff blonde boy was clearing the pool, calling, "Everybody out for twenty minutes! Twenty minutes!" He was about to throw some cleaning solvent around, but what he didn't know and I knew was that my kid was not going to budge. He was in the middle of his boat game and there would be no interruption without an enormous noisy battle involving all three of us.

I hopped in the water but I was many feet away from Will, calling out in complete and utter futility for him to come to me. The lifeguard, red-faced, was angrily scattering his crystals. "Get out, kid!" he yelled. "Get out of the pool right now!" The audience of families sat watching on the green banks, frozen like the pointillist figures of Seurrat. The hushed silence was broken by only one thing—the official announcement that came blaring from one little boy who was way out in the water, who was slowly and steadily raising one arm up in the air as if it were a crossing gate: "Now arriving, Bainbridge Island. Passengers please return to your vehicles now. Passengers: please enjoy your trip!"

He was one with his boat and there was nothing that could possibly mobilize him. No one on the real-world shore got it. They gaped at his mysterious performance. But I got it. And the tiny twinge of anxiety I felt as I again witnessed Will's expertise at finding ways to remove himself from the rest of humanity was nothing compared to how I felt in seeing his bliss at having an enormous pond to himself for his ferries. He stretched his arm up to the summer sky, lifting the imaginary gate. Deep down I know, when he honks his horn and revs up his engines, that we have actually come a step further. That a boat can show us the sea and the sea can introduce us to sea life, and maybe this is how we will be able to approach nature, and adventure, and science. And surely there must be other people interested in ferryboats. Slowly, over time, we will be able to use all this. The obsession will help us break through—I won't let it hold us back. He is fixated and it is abnormal, but although this may appear to be a window that is slammed shut, there is a crack where the light comes in—that just like any child who plays in an imaginary world Will is also in love.

The summer lifeguard gave up and worked around the ferryboat and the pond got its cleaning. A hundred kids jumped back in laughing and splashing and playing their own games, and the exceptional little boy blended right into the crowd again.

And now at the real dock a few seasons later, Will studies the carved wooden sign on the front of the boat that has just come in, the Kitsap. I watch the silver-white gulls hovering at the helm. They float and dip like little mascots, guiding the grand ferry into port. "Mom, is the Kitsap your favorite?" Will asks. A red and white gate rises and a ferry worker signals the cars to drive off. "They're all my favorites, honey," I tell him.

Potter vs. Potter

When I started my volunteer job working in the school library, on Wednesdays in the afternoon, I found myself handling the books as if they were treasures, holding each one like a coveted gift before I pushed it into its place on the shelf. Every now and then I'd glance around at the room with its walls of books and tall windows and feel a glow in my heart. I was a legitimate, bona fide elementary school mom.

Two years ago I'd been feeling rather helpless about Will's education. I believed we'd have to enroll him in a private school in order to get him the attention he required, but Will's dad and I went to look at many of those schools, the best, most expensive ones in Seattle, and none of them seemed to be equipped to handle all the stuff we'd be bringing with us. In the public schools, we found "special" classes, separated from the regular rooms, but we went to observe them and quickly knew that our son needed to be in a setting with typically developing kids, the way he had been in preschool. Finally we found Montlake, a public school not far from our neighborhood, an "inclusion model." We interviewed the Special Ed team there and found them very much to our liking. Of course, once we'd discovered this promising place we had to turn into political foxes, and audition like crazy to get in. But we were accepted. And things had gone okay. Will had, with much professional assistance, gotten all the way to the third grade in classes with regular children, where he often had an excruciating time keeping up. But, as usual, he rode high on his remarkable spirit and made it through.

I think back to the day I returned from the pediatrician's office, during the second year of Will's life, after the doctor had dropped the devastating news of his condition. The world was black, my beautiful little home with its pastel Peter Rabbit nursery and bright plastic toys strewn all over the floor seemed black, my whole life had changed during the course of a routine doctor visit. It was one of those visits that is supposed to mark your child's development, put him in a percentile bracket: the regular six-month "Healthy Child" meeting after which you feel fairly satisfied and go off with your baby to the park and play.

But the second the doctor's eyes met mine I felt the foundation of my life fall away. She had used the word "delayed" and when Charles and I came back to our house with me still trembling, I handed my baby boy his bottle, touched his curls with a brand-new tenderness, and went to my desk. I looked up "delay" in the dictionary, because I wanted the word to bail me out of all this. I wanted it to say, "A passing phase in development, applied to a mental condition and lasting only a short time." But it was not to be. Near the dictionary on my desk I noticed a newspaper catalog of schools I'd been perusing just the day before, still open to the page showing descriptions of some of our local private academies, with many of the names highlighted in yellow pen. Like all the parent overachievers I knew, I had been panicking, thinking we had to get on waiting lists right away, even though Will was only a little over two years old. For our only child, only the best would do.

But with the storm of information that was suddenly batting my mind around in what seemed like a whole new landscape, I was forced to make adjustment after adjustment in my thinking. I was being swept along a fast track. All my life I had looked upon the little universe of people with disabilities from my privileged window seat, but now I was being ejected from my spot and thrown right into the middle of it. When, after a couple of months, things at last settled down—after I'd written a hundred tear-stained pages in my journal, read everything there was to read on the subject of autism, spoken at length with professionals, and begun networking with mothers of little ones like mine—the sky cleared a bit and I saw what I was left with, what I had. A special boy, a wonderful boy. And a purpose in life. As a parent I had already figured out that I was going to have to try to be a teacher, but now I would need to hone my skills in a way I'd never imagined. A new strength pumped through my system like a steroid injection. After the grieving evolved into a new awareness, this power bestowed itself upon me like the sun. No matter what hardships came my way, I knew I'd be up to the task.

Yet along the journey there was always reason to keep a stiff upper lip, always a moment when I found myself forced to pluck up a certain amount of courage. Here in the Montlake Library this spring, it was Harry Potter. The Harry Potter books were sweeping the nation, the whole world. The kids in Will's class were devouring them. But Will's reading, his narrow interests, and his developmental "delay" created a giant impenetrable wall between his world and the world of J. K. Rowling. People who didn't know us that well seemed to be constantly asking me, "How does Will like Harry Potter?" and I wanted to say, "Will loves Pooh, Will loves Arthur and the characters from Sesame Street! Will adores the world of children's books! Does that work okay?"

On this particular Wednesday, as I filed away a couple of copies of *Charlotte's Web* and sorted through a stack of books on Egypt, I listened to two other volunteer mothers and the librarian discuss the new Harry Potter book that was to be released that summer. They mentioned characters from the previous stories, and brought up magical words and names I'd never heard before. "I'll bet Abigail just can't wait for the new one," said the librarian to one of the moms. "Is she excited?" The mother laughed. "What kid in third grade isn't?" she replied.

I thought I was beyond lumps in my throat, but I guess I wasn't yet. I thought I was beyond feeling the heavy heart of an outsider after glowing like a smug insider, and I was fairly sure I was beyond the envy, the longing. But this sort of thing still came up all the time, really. What was my kid not doing that all the other kids were? Well, most things. You've *got* to take him to see such and such movie, someone would say about the latest kiddie flick. But Will can't process the information that rushes past him on the silver screen. The movie theatre experience confuses him. Has he yet been to see a baseball game or any type of sports event? No. We drive by the big stadium all the time and he loves to see it, but once when we went past, he got a glimpse of the roaring crowd. That was enough for Will. A game, people, crowds, noise, chaos. Hot dogs, alien food, smells, sound that come out of the blue. No spectator sports yet. Videos? A few. But since he doesn't know what might come at him when the tape starts rolling, he nixes most titles most of the time.

And then, the reading issue. He certainly hasn't progressed as far as his classmates and does all his reading for class separately from them. The work he is given is tailored to his needs and his school does a wonderful job of helping him. I try to remember not to compare, just like all parents who tell themselves everything will come in good time. At moments I ache because I know how much he is missing. But there is no question that he is learning. He is following an uphill graph. His individual needs keep us from a lot of experience most of the time, but we *have* entered the world of books—though picture books and nursery books they may be, the land of literature has not left us behind. And as usual Will had to remind me of all this. Half the time, it is as if he wants to stop me in the midst of my worrying to say, "Listen, Mom. I'm doing okay."

A week after my library eavesdropping, Will came home from school, wolfed down his after-school snack and stood before me in the living room. "I'm going to read books!" he chirped. Since his reading level had not advanced much past first grade and was a source of frustration for his teachers and his parents, anytime he expressed enthusiasm in the book department everyone jumped to give him affirmation. "Hooray!" I cried. I dropped what I was doing and settled into the couch and waited for him to go to the bookshelf in his room. He came out with a pile of little pink and yellow and lavender books sliding around between his hands. *The Tales of Beatrix Potter*, his favorite stories of all-time. He'd begun memorizing them at age three and never let go.

He took his place in the chair. "Jeremy Fisher," he announced. He had always thought this story quite hilarious. "Once upon a time there was a frog called Mr. Jeremy Fisher; he lived in a little damp house amongst the buttercups at the edge of a pond." He studied each water-color as he went along. Jeremy Fisher fished and plashed and got into trouble. Will giggled. "The End!" he shouted and moved on. "The Tale of Peter Rabbit: Once upon a time there were four little rabbits." He couldn't wait to get to the part where Peter escapes mean Mr. McGregor. And so it went for more than an hour, a brisk, lively reading that, though I'd certainly heard it before, held my attention and was thoroughly entertaining. A journey through the pantheon of a different Potter.

He closed the last little cover. "I'm all done!" he grinned. He was so proud of his delivery of this delightful series, and pleased with his attentive mom. There are some strange and big words in those stories—"presently," "macintosh," "camomile"—and Will had pronounced them all beautifully. There is drama, which his passionate narration managed to capture. There is much humor—a fat little kitten whose mother is trying to stuff him into a suit, a frog who thinks he's going out to fish for minnows and instead pulls up Jack Sharp the Stickleback. It is sophisticated, brilliant stuff, actually, as every parent who sits down with it in the nursery is rather surprised to find out. In Will's case, familiarity is all. He loves these stories but he has also gone through each one of them probably two hundred times.

There will be time for the magic of Harry Potter, I realize now. So many things I've pined for have eventually come into Will's life, four or five years late. But these days the story that excites and enchants my still-little one involves a hilarious chase by a crotchety old gardener after a mischievous little rabbit who's lost his way. A huge bestseller, and a classic, world-famous storyline that's rarely been topped.

Into the Pool

Will can swim. He taught himself, though we tried to get him lessons. He went a few times to a wonderful teacher who worked with him one on one, but one evening he refused to return to his lessons—no big deal, he just didn't want to go back. He stole a few of the techniques he'd gotten from the teacher and created his own style. Now he swims in the deep end with his dad, and he'll even do a couple of laps. He floats. He plunges himself underwater and touches bottom. The minute he hits the pool he is as joyful as I have ever seen him.

Once in his preschool on the University of Washington campus, at the school that was a research site for child psychology, there was a big meeting of all the teachers and therapists to chart Will's progress and contribute suggestions for his improvement. The fact of this meeting amazed me—that without our even requesting a meeting we were going to be able to consult with experts from all sides on the subject of one thing—my child's education and welfare. There was some sort of buzz about one of the psychologists who would be in attendance. He was the big honcho in the Department of Psychology and knew a great deal about kids like Will, but his time was hard to book and everyone told me how excited I should be that he would be a part of the group. When the afternoon arrived, I had my eye on him. I couldn't wait to hear his comments. He listened to everyone talk and said nothing, but I could see that he was really, really listening. At last, after the doctor had heard everything there was to hear about this singular little boy, his turn came to speak. I leaned in toward him. He sat back, stroked his beard, looked at my husband and then at me, and one of his eyebrows went up. "He sounds like a pretty bright little boy and I think I have only one comment. As far as something that might be therapeutic—do you ever take him swimming?"

We hadn't, but we began to. There was a fabulous community pool right in our neighborhood. We thought that maybe the sound of screeching kids might put Will off, but the parents were the ones who, at the very start, needed earplugs. The shrieking sound during Family Swim Time could make for headaches. But none of the racket bothered Will, and as we watched him delight in the water, watched him take to it like a seal pup, it certainly no longer bothered us.

We go to the pool a couple of nights a week. And in the Olympic-sized turquoise pond where dozens of kids splash anonymously, where the wild shouts of swimmers bounce off the tile showers and concrete floors, where boys in goggles wrangle and wrestle each other in water games and beach balls of all colors bob up and down in between them, we are free. Not even the lifeguard notices that we're a little different than the rest. The blessed water lets us blend right in. There may be a moment when, floating on our backs and pretending we are the Wenatchee and the Walla Walla ferries, we stand out. But most of the time we can bump, flap, holler, squeal, be silly, lose our trunks, gurgle, wiggle, and shoot out of the water like rocket ships. No one pays any attention. And Will isn't paying attention to who's who either. I'm the one who really appreciates the anonymity, who looks out over the rippling blue and sees society in its most welcoming form. In Waterworld, everyone is the same.

Plus, the swimming solves a couple of problems for me. One is my resistance to pools, as a survivor of a potential drowning incident; I just sort of never got over a little dunking I had when I was eight. I've had no problem lying next to a pool in the sun of a tropical resort, but you'd never have caught me stuffing clothes in a canvas bag and heading off in the dark to get myself wet. Now, too bad, get over it, I'm there, I'm showering, I'm in and reviving the old breast stroke. Two is this nagging worry I've had about Will and sports. He doesn't do any team stuff. And the rest of the boys are all out there doing it, all the time. But there is life beyond soccer, you know, and we prove it twice a week as we practice and pump away and begin to look more and more professional.

The swim starts at seven in the evening, and Will is at the car door at 6:45. It doesn't matter about the weather. On one freezing winter night, the pool heater broke and the water was absolutely frigid. My son dove right in and began darting around like a guppy but I, California-girl-without-the-surfing-credentials that I am, could only stand there with water up to my knees, shaking. I'm sorry, I thought to myself, I don't think I can do this; I wish, I really, really, really wish I were home, right up next to a blazing fire, wrapped in a thermal blanket.

It took the longest time. Standing there like an idiot, at last I did become the object of people's attention. "I can't do it!" I whimpered. A couple of dads looked over and chuckled.

Meanwhile Will, sportsboy, athlete, self-taught slippery sea otter in blue goggles many waves away from me, was fed up. With a huge splatter he blasted himself up from the rippling surface. "Come on, Mama!" he yelled. "Get into the pool!" Once again, the water had liberated him: somehow he was suddenly able to shout out his request, like any regular kid. His spontaneity, so rare, and his sheer ability can on occasion just simply blow me away.

There was no choice but to take a big breath, squinch up my face, and go.

Afternoon on the Piazza

A warm, reassuring hand reaches over into the passenger seat of the car and clutches my own. There's no question: my husband's hand is the thing that gives me strength, that saves me, that is a great comforting gift in the midst of these mutual challenges of our lives. Here we are, holding on tight again on this still autumn afternoon, Charles and me, parked in front of the stately brick building that is Will's elementary school. I can almost hear the hum of little kids learning, sense the shuffle of papers and books from behind the windows of the classrooms, as the fall sun glints off the glass.

Charlie and I have this ritual of readying ourselves to walk bravely into yet another parent-teacher conference, a simple little hand-squeeze, a reminder that we're together in all this. We may be veterans of the scene now, but it is never easy to come face-to-face with the pros to discuss Will's primary education. In the days of his specialized preschool, it was different. The teachers seemed like our close personal friends, and together with them we formed one entity in the service of this terrific kid, feeling as jubilant about Will's progress as we were vigilant about facing his challenges. There was a fantastic feeling of company morale that made you think you were in a Frank Capra movie, since the whole focus of the place was on kids with enormous obstacles in their path.

Public elementary school has been a definite return to reality. The teachers and the principal are our allies, but they sometimes become overwhelmed by the magnitude of their responsibilities—they have so many goals to meet, so many young faces to remember in addition to our precious little one's, and they experience so much frustration. Charles and I sit in the last moments before the gathering trying to summon the strength to walk into the meeting room, because we know we are about to hear some of those frustrations voiced.

This particular meeting, however, began with more friction than we were ready for, and turned out to be one of the worst hours of my life. There were so many problems with Will as he entered third grade—his inability to focus on most subjects, his failure to grasp so many things combined with his stubbornness when he was asked to try to complete even a simple project—that I suppose certain people felt that someone had to be held to blame. Right away his teachers announced to us that as team members we "weren't following through"…that we were, in various ways, "sabotaging" some of the things they were trying to accomplish. This group of extraordinary women educators—and they are, that is why we have decided our son should be with them—felt that they were having to work beyond their capacity, and they blamed us.

I don't understand even now what the reasons were, but within minutes of the start of the meeting there were tears and high anxiety on both sides. It was them against us, or so it seemed to me in those first moments, and I just couldn't fathom how, with all we had to deal with at home, anyone could think we were a problem. At last I left the room sobbing, determined to jump in the car, drive to Canada, and leave them all there to work it out—the way I often would like to solve all our problems with school. But instead, I wandered the halls while Charles stayed and talked to everyone. He had collected himself after just a few moments of being shaken. He held up our side; I could hear him from the corridor where I was hiding, speaking evenly and convincingly to the group. He ended up being what he has been so many times before—the rock. I was able to go back in with a fistful of Kleenex I'd grabbed from the school office, and by then the climate of the room had changed. It seemed impossible that this meeting was able to continue, to be productive and get back to its focus—the wonderful little boy we all care about. But my husband had saved the day.

That strong hand—I knew there was something in it the first time Charles and I touched. I knew it on the day we married. But how could I know then of all the moments and days to come, when it would be necessary for that hand to rescue me?

★ ★ ★

Flash back a decade or more to the couple, in their glorious thirties, on honeymoon in Venice. I had started talking Charlie into a trip to Europe when we first met. We were musicians and music teachers and had no money, but he had never been to Paris or to London, and I was determined to take him to the cities I knew and loved. When things started getting serious it came together as a plan in my mind—the H-plan. The ultimate Honeymoon. What a dream it would be, traveling to all the romantic places as newlyweds. London, Paris, Florence, we decided. The Italian Riviera. And Venice.

We somehow pulled together the money it would cost, and, as late spring bloomed across Europe, we actually made the dream come true. There are scrapbooks to prove it. There we are there in Kodacolor: he with tousled hair, in trendy sport jacket, standing before a dazzling array of flowers on a Paris corner. She, in black sleeveless dress and barefoot, gazing dreamily into the camera from her window perch in a castle overlooking Portofino. At the end of the trip there was Venice. The first night we arrived, we were lost trying to find the restaurant and we ran across a million little bridges, laughing. The sunset and twinkle-lights popped up all around. On the canals, the gondolas were floating past as if ordered there by David Lean. The waiter at the restaurant brought us cannelloni from heaven.

The next morning we found a café and the perfect cappuccino and set off to explore the city. In the afternoon, thundering rains came down, and, with no umbrella, we had to huddle under an awning, freezing in our light spring clothes until it stopped. We hugged each other close, trapped in the doorway of a shop, and Charlie was grumpy. I clung to him and teased him. I sang him rain songs:

"Singing in the Rain," "Walking in the Rain," "Come Rain or Come Shine," every song about the rain I could think of until he started to smile. The showers finally stopped and the Italian sun returned in all its glory, warming up the cobbled streets again.

We wandered out onto the Piazza San Marco. The orchestras had just gotten underway. On one side of the plaza, twenty or so white-tuxedoed players and their lively conductor struck up a swing tune. From the other side, a second dance band sent out a waltz. Hundreds of pigeons exploded into the sky and flew past ancient spires, up toward Michelangelo clouds. We were lifted into another era; we suddenly became straw-hatted tourists in some other time. We sat in the sun sipping wine and watching the dancers, enjoying one orchestra and hearing faint horns and piano and drums from the other group across the way. And this is what I remember: Charles got up and took his camera across the square to take a photo of one of the bands. I watched him walk with his confident stride and I sighed like a teenage girl. Mamma mia, I thought, I've married the right guy.

When we got back home, we went round and round about whether or not to become parents. It took a couple of years to decide. In fact, we saw a counselor a few times and it was only after that series of visits with a professional that we could really say to each other that it was what we both wanted. It was a scary decision for us, for we knew the honeymooners would be left behind in the scrapbook, and the scrapbook would close.

When Will was diagnosed and I was falling apart, seeing the world through some sort of tunnel vision for a couple of weeks and having nightmares about my baby's future, Charles said, after a tear or two, "We'll get through this." And we have made it through, as a team. Charles is involved in every aspect of Will's brilliant career, from meetings with his therapists and teachers to helping him do homework to making sure he gets to the swimming pool every week to teaching him to ride a bicycle, and on and on. But it goes beyond the usual dad stuff. He has injected his son with his own sense of humor and fun; he has drawn Will out when Will seemed impenetrable. He has held him and brought him out of his strange, fearful episodes, when his world collapses in a way most of us can't understand, into a place that is safe and reassuring. He lavishes Will with affection whenever they are together. It is stunning to me, when I stop and ponder it, how much he is *there*.

And how unexpectedly it all unfolds. One moment, you and your lover are singing along in bad Italian with Venetians in a crowded bar, to accordion accompaniment on a moonlit night, red wine pouring out of nowhere. And the next minute, the two of you are filling out disability forms for your tiny son.

I once ran across a statistic saying that in families involving a child with special needs there is an 80 percent divorce rate. We steer a rocky ship, my husband and I. We are not always floating on a honeymoon canal. We have had to check in with the therapist, sometimes once a year, sometimes once a week. We've experienced a hard distance between one another from time to time, as Will in all his complexity takes over every spare second of our lives. We have hung on, though. Our hearts are bonded by something that goes even deeper than love.

★ ★ ★

I have shown William our photos of the Italian trip, and of Paris and the bustling streets of London. He loves them. He wants to know how you get to those places, how long it takes, which hotels have elevators. And when we turn the page to one particular snapshot, I usually force him to linger for a moment, because it's my favorite picture, the only one taken of Charlie and me together during our European trip, after we actually got up the nerve, using crazy gestures, to ask an Italian hotel owner to snap the photo. The starry-eyed couple sits at a cafe table in the light, with butter-yellow walls behind them, and hanging vines of luminescent green. They are grinning like romantic fools, and his hand covers hers.

Singer

I'm sitting here listening and it is unmistakable. It's a lovely, lilting, lyrical voice I'm hearing. It's a singing voice. It's Will's voice. Yet it's my voice.

It's coming from the bath, as it often does now. His pitch is truer than mine, I notice, and throughout the entire performance his energy and spirit pretty much put to shame the so-called sparkle of his show business mom. Whether it's a Neil Diamond number he learned while listening to the oldies station in the car with his dad (and at this moment it is: "Thank the Lord for the Nighttime"), or a classical choice, like "Waltz of the Flowers" from the Nutcracker Suite (a robust version of which he was caught humming a few times during the holidays), well, what can I say. The guy has the same pleasing tone that helped me coast through many a vocal competition. The guy can sing.

He pumps away, warbling and crooning as the faucet runs, and even though he started singing a year or so ago, I still put down the book I'm reading and cock my ears in disbelief. I can't help but pay serious attention to every nuance, every note. By god. His father and I, both professional musicians, once watched him stand stock still in a little kindergarten chorus during a program for the parents in his first year at public school. He was silent. The other kids all sang brightly, levitating with pride, while Will stood mute, his eyes darting around the room. Every now and then he would jump up and flap. He knew what was going on, he was loving the music. But he could not sing.

Then one evening one year later, he recreated the kindergarten program note-for-note in the tub. He sang every word of every song in perfect tune. During that school performance, a stabbing heart-pain had forced a sob from my throat, when Will could not sing the sweet finale, "Oh What a Beautiful Morning," with the rest of the children. And I cried again from my living room chair when he finally did sing it, in his own good time, twelve months from downbeat, in the bathroom on a beautiful night.

The autism consultant who came to our house heard him vocalizing and said, "They don't usually sing!"

Yet I was exactly Will's age, a little trooper of nine, when I made up my mind that I would be a singer when I grew up. I used to put on my roller skates after school, hit the sidewalk and race around the block as Disney tunes and Shirley Temple songs rose from my kid's heart up into the warm Southern California air. I knew singing would be my life. When I became a mother I desperately needed to feel that my child would have music. But when William was four years old and still not talking, I thought—okay, put that dream away. Get a nice sturdy lock and toss out the key.

Something was too powerful, though, to stay locked away. I showered him with the tunes of my childhood, with songs of the Beatles, with classical and jazz and Broadway melodies. I was in his face from the time he was an infant, and although he couldn't coo back, he got it. He latched onto our CD collection, literally—he was one and a half when he started chewing on the booklets and the jewel cases, and got into a regular habit of spinning the discs on the floor. But he let us play them for him too, as he sat in a mysterious trance in front of the stereo speakers.

As with all the information William struggles to process, who knows how these sounds reached him, how they may have touched him and simmered somewhere deep inside, mixing all together and coming out of him at last? His father is one of the top jazz musicians in our city, and the sound of Papa practicing his upright bass rings through the rooms of our home nightly. My teaching practice brings a parade of voice students into the house and from babyhood Will would giggle at the funny-sounding exercises that floated through the air—ming ming ming, loo loo loo. It is all around, it is everywhere, it is our life. But for so long Will seemed incapable of giving us the gift we dreamed of. Now, recently, we've received shocking reports from his teachers: he was actually caught singing Christmas carols in a new school chorus the other day. There is a band for fourth and fifth graders, and our arts-oriented school principal has suggested that we try starting Will on an instrument. The fantasies that were so fleeting, that seemed so out of this mother's grasp once upon a time, now light on my shoulder and stay for a moment, like amazing little butterflies that I may someday be able to hold in my hand.

All I know is that now the songs pour out of him, out of the soul of a person who can still go very stiff when trying to formulate a request, or an idea, or even a simple greeting. There is a different channel, a magic channel, for his music. The repertoire is diverse. Miles Davis (he sings the trumpet solos). Jimi Hendrix. The best of Rodgers and Hammerstein and the best of Bach. We are way beyond the nursery songs of kindergarten now and exploring the classics, as well as the greatest of twentieth century pop. There is no end to it, and my little singer is in his glory. The first thing he does on waking every day is ask me to sing him a song, which I guarantee he will have down pat in a version of his own by day's end.

Another tub time. A splish and a splash and the voice sounds again. "I've been working on the railroad!" it rejoices. "All the livelong day!!" Still on the edge of her chair, the one-woman audience swoons. And thinks to herself—oh, what a beautiful morning.

Friends

I had a goal growing up, and the goal was to find a friend.

For some reason I couldn't find any for years. Maybe it was the fact that I was an only child who was moved around by my parents eight or nine times before I reached the age of seven. There was a pivotal moment in my first grade class, a class I was a part of for only a couple of months before we moved again, which is etched in my mind. The LA sun beat down on the playground. I had managed to luck out, and cute blonde Debbie with the nice dresses had allowed me to attach myself to her. I knew I'd scored. We were walking arm-in-arm across the blacktop at recess, long ponytails bouncing. A boy called out in a singsong voice, "Deb-bie's pret-ty, Kel-ly's pret-ty!" Debbie and I skipped away, laughing. Did I know Debbie for a day, a week? Yet I can still see her blond hair, her face, her fresh blue-and-white-checked blouse.

And I remember that very soon after that day my parents announced we were moving to Oregon.

I felt like I was standing on shaky ground every time I entered a new school situation, and I entered a new one with the turn of every semester. Shyness wrapped around me like a straitjacket. I was, I now realize, hurting with loneliness. And to make things worse, I was completely uncoordinated. In each new grade, as soon as I tapped the tetherball or tried awkwardly to kick the kickball, my reputation in school spread as quickly as wildfire. I was the Cootie Bug.

In third grade, we settled for good back in Los Angeles, but it took me four more years to hit the jackpot. Her name was Bonnie and we met in seventh-grade math class. Suddenly, by accident, I had magic back in my life. We had the Beatles, old movies from the Thirties and Forties, clothes, boys, everything in common. Bonnie, far more savvy than me in the land of friend-getting, helped us devise a plan to capture kindred spirit Linda, and soon, with the addition of Kathy and Francie, it was a gang of five. A life-changing chain reaction had begun out of nowhere and I came into a completely new world, a place where I began to understand that I could actually own a bit of power. No more Cootie; I was loved. I could walk the halls of middle school with protection and pride. The Gang of Five is now, thirty-five years later, spread out around the world, and four of us are still in close contact. All the confidence I have in the universe came from them.

Life became infinitely easier once I had friendship. But I can remember thirsting for it, dreaming of it, praying for it with all my might before it came.

Now the course of my life has taken me backwards. Back to the praying and the longing. Back to experiencing the isolation that stings so sharply. For here I am with William, a little person straitjacketed himself by a condition that is guaranteed to shut him out of the society of others; the social hardwiring simply isn't there, as one of his docs once told me. He is ten years old, and he hasn't got a friend. It is as if he doesn't notice his peer group. When forced into looking at them, he has no idea what to say or what to do. He must be programmed and prompted to play with them, and reprogrammed with each new kid. And this, of course, is hard on the other kid, who soon gives up on Will. I stand in the corner with him, remembering.

But our struggle is so much bigger than mine was, and all around our house you will see signs of it. A Polaroid tacked to the kitchen bulletin board shows Will sitting stiffly at a table in a therapy room across from another little boy. The caption, written in magic marker by the therapist, says, "Will and Kevin are just right." This photo came from a six-week course in how to have a conversation. Because all four kids in this special class had a tendency to move right up close into the other person's face when trying to communicate, they spent an hour learning just how far apart they should be from one another when talking. Pull out one of our desk drawers and you are likely to see notes in computer print from other sessions. "What do I do when I see someone I know? a) run away b) hide behind Mom c) say 'Hello'."

I had trouble making friends as a child. But with Will's life, we are always starting over, again and again, with the very basics.

The truth of it all is that once more, the pain belongs to me. I think—I believe—that Will doesn't notice that he is lacking, that his life is missing the gift that most kids have, just by nature, happened upon. Due to his intense early education and the commitment and love of the adults who surround him, he has learned to communicate freely with his parents and babysitters and aunts and uncles, and he has made great strides. These friends have patience. They will wait 120 seconds for the first words to form from Will's lips. They will answer his repeated questions, and allow him to speak on the same limited subject over and over again, if they feel that it's the only way to get the spark of communication going. There has been reward for him in trying to connect with these grown-up pals, so he has gotten much better, more confident at allowing his personality to come out. So for now, the adults in Will's world, especially his father and me, are his friends.

I watch life go by, with other families' sleepovers and birthday parties and soccer games, and from my own window see childhood unfolding in our kid-happy neighborhood: two toddlers rolling down the street together on their tricycles, balls being bounced back and forth between kindergartners, kites flying, laughter and crying and shouts and the calling out of names—Joshua! Alex! Olivia!

When I was small I used to wait to hear another child say my name, and now I wait for someone to call out for Will. When I'm not waiting I am an activist, finding ways to bring other children into our lives. My attempts at birthday parties for Will have been heroic. He has seemed to want them, and I've done everything in my power to make them happy for him, but when the guests arrive he usually leaves—he walks out the door and sits on the sidewalk, while the others whoop and holler in their paper hats with frosting on their fingers. It happens whether I create a perfect plan to invite a gang or just two willing classmates, whether I leave it up to chance or clear every last tiny detail with the honoree, whether I keep things quiet and calm or let the whole thing explode into the more normal child-driven racket.

We try playdates, too. The ones that take place at our house yield nothing except one antsy little host who wants to quit the whole idea, and one frustrated guest who wishes he had someone to play with. Visits to the homes of other children, planned and prepared for weeks in advance ("This is what the house will look like...Here is what we'll say when we come in the door"), don't usually last longer than twenty minutes. Will recoils from his playmate's unpredictable advance. The stimuli of the new place overwhelms him. At first it is as if he wants to go to the kid's house, wants to be able to play, but it soon becomes apparent that he is very uncomfortable. Often the other mother gets involved trying to assist him right alongside me and we come up with all sorts of ideas—toys that will engage him, holding him in our laps and massaging him while he gets used to the environment. But the most valiant attempts end in failure.

There are little moments of progress in his school life. According to the teachers and staff who observe him, he spends his recess time alone, sits by himself at lunch, and takes long bus rides on field trip days without exchanging one word with anyone else on the bus. Yet when he is forced into some social exchanges at school, he seems to delight in them. Often other kids are assigned to help him at his desk. He will sometimes partner with a kid in P.E. Most of these elementary school children who come into contact with him are sweet and kind, and happy to discover that they have what it takes to help William. Little do they realize that they are giving him an enormous gift—the important peer contact he regularly lacks.

Meanwhile, Will is content to play at home on his own, to pretend he is a ferryboat pushing across the imaginary Puget Sound of our den, with a dock he has meticulously made from blocks and Legos and pillows. He is alone and he is happy, as long as I am nearby. Heaven forbid any brazen child should make an attempt to share in this game. It is a one-man operation.

I'll watch him play, and it will take me a week or so to muster up the energy, but then I'll pick up the phone again. For, while he seems oblivious to other kids, I am always on the case, searching for a match. I find out from Will's teacher which of the other students are sensitive to him, which ones might be helping him in class. There have been quite a few over the years who are intrigued by Will's persona, who think he's "cool," and though they have not ended up as playmates, whenever I find out about them hope rises up in me, hope I can barely contain. At his summer camp last year, I saw Will arm-in-arm with another boy. The boy's name was Roger. I made certain to get Roger's phone number. Maybe Roger needed a friend too. But somehow I never managed to get the two boys back in the same room together. I usually don't give up that easily, but there are times when even I run out of steam, trying to pull the Friendship Train.

And it may end up to be a long haul. When the Gang of Five went their separate ways and I moved from Los Angeles to Seattle, I continued to go after friendship the way other people chase after money. I wanted to be rich with friends. Into my twenties and thirties I was lucky enough to find more treasure. In a way I happened upon it, but in many ways I also made it happen. I know how to be a friend now. There are rules, just like the rules I've had to script for my son. I'm famous these days for my birthday parties overflowing with warm, radiant women—my best friends. The ones who understand that, though I may not always be able to give them everything the friendship needs because I am so busy giving to someone else, I am a true and loyal heart that will always stay that way, having taken a whole childhood to go from empty to full.

People who know my family or who have observed our home life sometimes suggest to me that I let Will have too much control—over his environment and over me. I agree with them. He wants me to watch every pretend ferryboat run and sit next to him while he watches videos; he wants to tell me when I can and can't play music in the house and he wants to tear up our living room and move all the furniture around to build boat docks. But in so many areas of his life he must still stay so far in the background, with no way, yet, to speak for himself. He can't have a simple argument with a buddy over a game, or shout instructions to a teammate on the soccer field. He has no one his size to laugh with. Until he has that one friend who makes him feel he could conquer the world, I let him conquer me a little. Maybe it helps me with thoughts of the past that keep resurfacing when I look at him. I only want him to be able to enjoy, even for a few moments, the sense of beautiful, benign power that it is possible to feel, just by being yourself with another person who cares about you.

The Lunchmaker

Oh so long ago, when I was in my early twenties, I remember reading a fluffy little pop questionnaire in a fashion magazine. It was titled something like, "Who Are You—Really?" and asked a series of questions designed to help all us early-twenties girls figure out what would bring us the most satisfaction in life. Do you like to draw? Are you good at math? One of the questions caused me to ponder, and is the whole reason I even recall this silly little survey. "Are you an 'appreciator' of the arts, of food, of people?" That question took so much pressure off a struggling young woman—it made me feel that maybe I could actually play a role in the big world of Life, just going around appreciating things. To that interview question, the answer was an automatic, enthusiastic "Yes!"

I don't remember how the upside-down-on-the-page results came out, but it doesn't matter now. I've discovered who I really am, though it took longer than I'd have imagined way back then. I have found the title by which I want to be known, the job that fulfills me more than any other ever has or possibly could. I am a Lunchmaker.

That twentysomething girl I once was, that girl who came of age at the beginning of the dawn of feminism—the one who swore she'd never have kids—would never have believed it. She'd have tsked and rolled her eyes in disgust at the thought of packing someone's PB and J every morning of the working week. But it is a long way for a woman from the twenties to the forties, a complicated journey involving many big surprises, and moments of enlightenment (hopefully), and, for some of us, marriage and motherhood. I experienced my first favorite job when I walked down the aisle at age thirty-six: Bride. It was so great to be a Bride, but it was a temp job, lasting only a few hours at the end of a few months of training. Pregnant Person, another good job, turned out to be a relatively short one as well—that's how it felt for me, anyway. The position of Lunchmaker, by contrast, should hold up for quite a few years.

It was on my son's first day of kindergarten that I got my new calling. Before that, William attended a preschool with a short schedule, and the school provided his midmorning treat. Now I was readying him for the big time. The lunchbox had been carefully chosen for size and color (royal blue). The menu was a collaborative creation and easy to decide upon since Will would only eat five or six things, and crackers and peanut butter sandwiches were high on the list. (This is a situation that still exists, as food is another intruder that can be a terrible affront to his senses—he quickly turns his head away from most things offered.) And so it was all set. I rose on the morning of that first day with great pride and excitement. We were headed off into the big world, and as I packed, things fell blissfully into place. The thermos fit in the middle of the box, between the crackers and the sandwich. The napkin lay on top. All items had been checked previously for easy opening, since little fingers were still in the course of being helped by occupational therapy. On the front of the lunch box I had printed perfectly in indelible ink—"Will, Room 2." My heart soared.

Every school day since then, the yellow-and-black chariot has come to carry Will off. This is the little van-sized Special Ed bus with just a few kids riding and always with an actual bona fide saint driving. We have fallen in love with our school bus drivers, our Kathies and Elliotts and Yvonnes, over and over again, for now we have had four years of throwing our lunch into our backpack, hiking the whole thing up over our shoulder, and tromping up the bus steps into our seat. And you can imagine by now how seriously expert I am at the lunchmaking gig.

There is anticipation every day when you have a kid who's the only challenged one in his class of twenty-six. As I unscrew the lid on the peanut butter jar, as I pour just the right amount of juice into the thermos, as I take a break from doing the lunch and run around to gather clean underwear and socks, I wonder about the boy's coming day. Once Will's lunch was stolen right from under his nose, something so easily accomplished by kids who knew they can get away with it. He could not report it, or ask for something else to eat. There have been official reports by the teaching staff of Will being taunted by the other kids with name-calling and pushing, and unofficial ones—such as the time a little girl in the hallway ran up to tell me, "I wish the other kids would stop saying bad things to Will." The teachers are on the lookout; the students are generally sweet and kind. But even when questioned at the end of his day, William can't formulate sentences well enough to tell me anything about school; or else he refuses to, in his not-so-atypical desire to keep home separate from the classroom. What goes on there, every day, that a mother can't know about?

On a few occasions the staff has called me in, wringing their hands because they don't know what to do with my son, they don't know how to teach him, they're getting nowhere. And I have stood before them, helpless, weeping. When the road turns rocky like this I understand the value of a ritual. I understand that my preparation of Will's sustenance for the day is almost like a prayer. I can't jump in and remake his world. I can busy my hands though, in a regular task designed to please him and make him feel safe, and somehow in the little moments of doing it I can feel safe too.

In spite of all the dangers, and of the times when he has languished in the classroom and seemed somehow unreachable, William mostly carries himself proudly through his elementary school days. He does extremely well in the math department. With assistance, he has been known to fly through standardized tests. He roller skates in the gym, he goes happily on every field trip, he reads aloud before his class. Every day gets better. I was so filled with joy over his progress one fateful Friday that I decided to do the cute mom thing and write a little note on his lunch napkin and put a piece of candy next to his sandwich. He came home angry, his food uneaten. The surprise presentation had upset him. He was not expecting it.

So I strive to keep it simple and the same, Monday through Friday, morning in, morning out. It is my contribution to Will's large, looming schedule. It's one of the ways we hold it all together. My maternal love seeps into the project with every stroke of the spreading knife, with every careful sealing of every baggie, with the last confident motion that zips the whole thing together. Every morning when I get up I know who I am, really. Every day, with a purpose and gratefulness beyond anything I ever dreamed I could possess, I make my little boy's school lunch.

Big Talk

I'd thought about the moment for a long time, and on that spring morning the moment suddenly arrived, barely giving me any choice. I was going to have to find the words to tell Will about his differences. I'd been waiting for the day when a miracle would tumble down from heaven on the rays of the sun, when he would suddenly start looking and acting like everyone else and I wouldn't have to tell him anything at all. I wouldn't have to write the speech of my life. But that day hadn't arrived.

We were having fun on the school playground under a cloudless blue sky. Will was playing his "bridge game"—using a walkway on the play structure to recreate every bridge he had ever seen in the state of Washington—and I was settling in happily and comfortably to watch. Then, out of the blue, came the jarring, clanging sound of the school bell. It was supposed to be turned off today, on a Saturday. I know this to be the rule better than anyone else knows it because I make regular phone calls and talk to school officials about when the bells will ring and when they won't. I don't know what went wrong. Of the many things that can take the air out of my kid, harsh-sounding bells that come with no warning are right at the top. When they sound, he goes directly into spasms. He falls apart with fear. He shakes and cries uncontrollably. I rush to hold him with all my might.

I sometimes operate like a kind of machine in these sorts of situations, switching to autopilot to comfort and console and turning off when it's all over. But today I leave my nerve endings exposed, today I feel all the pain—pain from what? a bell!—that there is to be felt. Rage wells up inside me. When Will was diagnosed, a close friend, a parent, asked "Aren't you raging?" I had no anger then, only a mother warrior's keen drive to go further into the jungle to find the beast and either calmly and tidily kill it or find a way through my desperation to befriend and understand it, and talk it into leaving our family territory. But today I feel another native instinct as I sit here on a wooden park bench mentally shaking my fist at the sky. A bell rang and my child went into spasms and fell to the ground in tears. I have had it with all this. It happens all the time, and we are so tired and so weary and we've traveled so far through clinics and therapy rooms and hospitals and special schools to solve this sad mystery—the mystery of the shock and reverberating pain that comes from a school bell, and countless other random sounds and movements of everyday life.

"Honey, honey, honey," I say as I gather him up off the ground. "Come here, come here, let's sit on the bench together and talk about it."

He is sobbing. "Talk about it," he says.

"Well, we weren't expecting the bell were we? The bell was supposed to be turned off and somehow, suddenly, it must have rung by accident!"

"Yeah." Shaking.

"I don't know why it happened, but I am going to call the school and find out."

"When?"

"Tomorrow."

"No tomorrow."

"All right, I'll do it as soon as we get home"—knowing I will have to fake the call since all the schools are closed today. And this ends the standard portion of comforting words and hugs, the part I have down pat. Now my hug becomes tighter, closer. I feel my breath in his tousled hair.

"Will, do you ever wonder why you get so scared when something comes out of the blue, why it upsets you so much?"

He sniffles. "Yeah."

I hesitate. I'm feeling terribly warm. I never wanted to introduce my child to the label someone else created for him. And yet an instinct tells me it may help him, give him something to cling to for a moment. "Do you remember a couple of times when mom was talking to one of your teachers or therapists I've used that word that starts with an 'A'—'autism'?"

"Which teacher?"

"Well, one or two different ones, I've used that special word. That word describes something you may have been born with. You have something inside you that makes you—well, it makes you get a shock when things happen—when they happen unexpectedly." I am tripping over stones on a strange and difficult trail, picking and sidestepping my way through the underbrush.

And now he's still. He has calmed down. He's listening.

"And sometimes when you feel like you're different from the other kids in your class, that's why it is. It's something called autism that the doctors told us about when you were two years old. It is something we work with and we try to help all the time but sometimes it gets hard. Do you feel sometimes that it's hard, and that things are a little bit different for you than for other kids?"

Stillness. "Yeah."

And silence, as I try to imagine where to go next. Maybe I'm all wrong. Maybe I should never have used that word. But an odd rush comes over me. It feels like, with this tentative back-and-forth, we've suddenly crashed through some floodgate. I feel like a jazz musician who is playing a down and sorrowful blues but all at once finds herself improvising on some unexpected soaring riff, filled with release. Has Will known for awhile that he has a problem; has he been waiting for his mom to explain it to him? There is in all this talk something for both of us to hold onto, maybe in this one moment a way to quell the terror, or even rise above it.

"Papa and I are finding ways to help you. We are always finding ways to help you, that's the good thing. That's why you've had so many therapy classes. That's why you have special teachers at school.

And some day...." A sigh I've been harboring escapes my throat. "Someday all the horrible parts will go away."

"All the horrible parts will go away," he repeats. He is rapt with attention, so unusual. I wonder if I'm telling the truth or if in my passion to comfort him I have just burst forth with a gigantic lie. But it feels like I am simply imparting my own beliefs. I do believe the horrible parts will go away. That is how I've held on during this roller coaster ride, and I want him to learn how to hold on too.

"Do you understand what I am saying?" He's been listening to me even though he's been protecting his ears with his hands the whole time.

"Yeah." We hug tighter.

"And so we can get up and go home now, now that we've talked about this. We can have some lunch and play inside in our nice cozy home."

"Yeah."

"Are you ready to get up?"

He jumps up and runs as fast as he can to the car, hands still over his ears, and I sprint after him. The sun is growing warmer. We hop quickly through a children's garden where bright green sprouts are coming up in rows from dark, moist soil. We run to our car, away from bells, away from surprises, away from fear.

The King

Escalatorland

Will is turning six, and I'm getting pretty excited about this year's birthday cake. I think I've figured out how to do it: I'll start with a pound cake, and get it angled at a slant somehow, and start carving. Silver food coloring? They must sell it somewhere. And black licorice for the rails, and a new comb to make grooves in the frosting, and, oh yes, a red gumdrop for the emergency button and…my god, it's happened. I've gone insane. I've joined my son in Escalatorland.

I was the one, after all, who really got into it when I decided that it was finally time for Will to create his own birthday party idea. In the past I had always been the theme-thruster—pushing Pooh, touting Thomas the Tank Engine, strong-arming Sesame Street, as Will went cheerfully with the flow. Now out of courtesy and respect, I asked him what he wanted and out popped the concept for which neither Hallmark nor Disney could provide any assistance whatsoever: "I would like an Escalator Party," he grinned.

It's interesting to me that I so quickly accepted this vision, considering the fact that I once despised the big rolling monsters. After a lifetime of barely noticing them, they suddenly began to loom large in my parenting life, for they possessed the power to take my child's mind away from anything a kid would normally love. Up and up, hand-in-hand he and I would go, whenever the people-carrying machine appeared before us. Away from the world we'd float: past the F.A.O. Schwartz windows gleaming with day-glo; up, moving by the colorful garden of kiddie books at Barnes and Noble; up, up, into oblivion, leaving behind the ice cream, the popcorn, the clowns and balloons in the Seattle Center Food Circus—all of the wonders of childhood disappearing below as we continued our slow, steady ascent to nowhere.

From the time he was two, nothing could attract Will like the magical motorized staircase. Like Richard Dreyfuss moving toward the mothership as the *Close Encounters* theme chimed, Will would see the shining steps and head for outer space. And I knew that I was riding in the midst of a controversy: should the parents and therapists of these small addicts let them have their fixations and try to use the deified item as a learning tool, as some professionals in the world of autism advise? Or should we force the children, in a different form of therapy, to go cold turkey, and strictly point them in another direction? Kids like mine will take their narrow interests to bizarre extremes; they will so deftly figure out ways to block out the real world. When you find yourself walking through life holding hands with one of them, their single-mindedness takes you by surprise and has you anxiously wondering which way to pull. If I can, I try to yank him away, turn him around, but his determination and rigidity can make this a superhuman task, and there have been many failed attempts.

One day as my son and I stood perched at the top of yet another landing, with Will jumping and flapping as excitedly as a climber who'd reached the summit of Everest, I knelt at his side in desperation. "Will!" I implored in a harsh whisper, gripping his little arm. "There's more to life than escalators!" But he took my hand and stepped on, and by the time we'd arrived at the next floor of that particular department store he was crowing to the shoppers at top volume: "There's more to life than escalators! There's more to life than escalators!" And as folks peered over at us with curious expressions, I began to dream of automatic stairs that could lift me through the roof.

Eventually, though, I began to understand their calming effect. When the stress of life becomes too much, as it does each day for Will, wouldn't I myself seek out the hypnotic release of the Pacific Ocean if I saw that it was available in every downtown bank building? Will had found the relaxation method that was perfect in every way. It never changed. It couldn't come at you from left field—like nature, or a human. If there was an up one there was a down one and if there was a down one there was an up one. The symmetry and regularity could only be disrupted in the event of a power outage, or if somebody got their shoestring caught.

So in the most child-centered style of surrender, I literally went along for the ride. Through department stores and office buildings, hotels and hospitals, shopping malls and airports and bus tunnels, we blazed our vertical trail. I tried my best to educate along the way. We noticed skylights above our heads, babies riding with us, numbers and letters that marked our path. But somewhere between floors my peda-gogical stance got wiped out. I found myself wondering about the escalator's innards (which we once got to glimpse during a thrilling moment with repairmen at a local hospital), its history (who invented it? In what year?), and its manufacturers (Otis and Haughton are two proud names one often sees engraved at the foot). I imagined the Mid-western escalator factory we might visit one day in a distant burg like Oshkosh or Fargo. I even pictured mother and son getting together to beat a Guinness record—so many escalators in so many days in so many cities. The two of us, weary but grinning for the media, at the last plateau in some supermall in Canada.

And so the birthday cake, a monument to our travels, but, when I come back down to earth, something I suppose I'd rather think of as a milestone to build and leave behind. There's got to be a way for Wil-liam and his mom to get over this, or at least branch out. I thought of a new title for Will's celebration and it seems to check out OK with him: Things That Go Up and Down. This way, in addition to the original and amazing cake, we can include yo-yos, bouncing balls, and swings, to the relief of our party guests, no doubt. And perhaps these varia-tions on a theme will one day allow my little guy to see that, like the waves that roll up and hit the sand, like the sun that rises and sets, in the scheme of things, there's more to life than escalators.

Candy

I know why I let the kids take those little chocolate bars and peel the
foil away with their tiny, nimble fingers. I know exactly why I allowed
them to eagerly pop the candy into their mouths on that bright, blus-
tery morning a few days before Halloween, the morning that now
seems so long ago. I never tried to tell myself, or anyone, any differently. I knew why I was doing it, at the moment that I did it.

Will was two. We were enrolled in a little cooperative preschool
with a wonderful teacher named Karen Truelove. She was a love, and
in our neighborhood she had become somewhat of a legend—to get
your kid into Karen's class, where there was a waiting list every fall,
was to have your toddler starting his or her education with the best.
We were lucky to make it into the little school called Springbrook. It
was a painted blue portable box sitting right next to a stream, with a
bridge leading over the water to the kids' playground. On the Introduction Night, when I walked up the wooden ramp to the door of the
portable and peeked in to get my first glimpse of the classroom, I was
charmed: there were rows of little artist's easels, trays of alphabet
blocks and jars of play-dough on small portables, and a loft that contained a library of children's books. I felt a fantastic sense of privilege.
Will and I went to school every Tuesday morning. On Thursday
nights he went with his dad. It seemed like it was going to be perfect.

But things didn't work out as I had hoped. Will wasn't able to be a
part of the preschool program. He didn't participate in any of the
games or songs; he didn't want any of the playthings. He marveled at

an exit sign above the doorway. He ran away from story circle, as far as he could get from the others in the large classroom group (twenty-two little people plus parents). The loft library was his hangout and he huddled there through most of class time. He couldn't sit in his chair during snack; I had to chase him around the room to get food in his mouth. (I was always chasing, chasing and capturing and holding, at Springbrook.) When it was time to go out to the playground he found the tube slide, crawled in and stayed there. No one could get him to come out. The other parents glanced over at us and glanced away. Every Tuesday morning, as it turned out, my heart started filling with dread, and the little songs and stories of nursery school sent me into unidentifiable, silent resentment.

It was in this setting that Karen Truelove and another teacher brought Will's differences to my attention (not that they hadn't already begun to stand out before my own eyes—but the truth was the hardest thing to see). A neurologist was called, the beginning of a life of paperwork and testing and hopes and fallen hopes began. And after the anguish, confusion and indescribable heartache, there came a deep feeling of relief and understanding, which in the end left me ever grateful to that preschool staff. But all of this took place after the day of the candy.

We had made it through the first two frustrating months of school to the end of October. On the day of my terrible lapse in judgment the class was having their playground time and Will was, as usual, stuck in the tube slide. The wind blew everyone's hair around in the sun.

I wandered over to a trio of two-and-a-half-year-olds cheerfully playing in the gravel. The experience I was going through, of trying so hard to fit in and never being able to find a way, made me look upon other children with awe, as if they were even more magical and wondrous than they actually are. I was attracted to them, like the unpopular girl in school who observes the cool kids. I saw how they communicated with each other, how they handled toys; they all seemed like little geniuses to me. The close day-to-day experience with my own preschooler was so drastically different. For one thing, there was no speech yet. And I would have no luck at all introducing a stuffed animal, a dish of ice cream. My little boy obstinately refused them, refused the fun of life, and was happiest when I handed him a pot lid so that he could spin it for minutes on end on the kitchen floor. He was not interested in much else. I could never seem to sit him down and convince him, yet I tried each day, with every desperate ounce of motherly energy I possessed.

Suddenly there came a happy cry from one of the kids, a little girl who had toddled a few feet away from me, to the edge of the playground. "Look over here!" she called. "Candy!" The two boys at my feet scrambled over to her. "Candy, candy," they cheered. Propped up against a little stone statue of a rocket ship was a Halloween treat bag, sitting in the dirt, a treasure appearing out of nowhere. It was shiny black and orange, it appeared to be untouched, it looked completely and legitimately Hallmark—it looked like fun. In an instant and before I knew it—because I had no idea how fast little children like this could go to work—all three of them were grabbing at it and unwrapping chocolate like crazy. And that was when, for me, things started moving in slow motion. I saw them eating it, I saw their hands getting messy, I saw them fighting over it and laughing and jumping around with glee. It was like a lovely scene from a film, with me playing the mother. And I didn't want to stop them; I wanted to watch them. I wanted to be a part of giving them this joy. I longed, from the deepest part of me, to give it to them. I didn't really think or care how the bag had gotten there. I know I must have been smiling.

The shadow of a frantic mom blocked the light. "What are you doing?" she yelled over the wind, "What's happening here? Where did that bag come from?" It was Halloween, for god's sake, the bag could have come from anywhere. There was a high school right across the street. I was yanked out of my reverie. I was suddenly nauseous with embarrassment.

The kids were herded back to class by some of the other parents. Karen Truelove arrived on the scene and I uttered something like, "They got to it before I could stop them, I'm so sorry, I'm so sorry." My desperate dream of making a little one happy came to an end in a moment shot through with fear. "Go home," said Karen. "I'll call you."

I gathered Will and his things and put him in the car. I looked at him. Oh, how I loved him. I would never want anyone but Will. I knew I could expect to hear from the parents of the children I had been supposedly standing guard over. I knew what they would think of me.

I was at home sitting in a daze when Karen called. "The parents of two of the kids are okay," she told me in a solemn voice on the phone, only an hour after I had left her. She'd gotten on the case right away, trying to calm the parents, calling the playground people and the high school to find out what kind of trick or treat stuff had been officially passed around. Black and orange bags, matching the description of the one I had allowed to be ripped open by the joyful babies, had been offered that morning at the nearby community center. But one father of a little boy was really upset. He wanted to talk with me. He would be calling.

Minutes later the low voice at the end of the line tried to control the emotion behind it, as this father spoke to me of the potential consequences of my actions. I remembered that he and I had once enjoyed a jovial conversation in the classroom, but now the jokes were over. It was still too early to tell if the chocolate had been left by a prankster, if it had been laced with something dangerous, and the dad's tone was understandably unforgiving. "What if my son has to go to emergency? What if he starts coughing up blood? Couldn't you see what you were doing, how dangerous that was?" He asked me question upon question as he got up his nerve, trying to find out from this idiot woman how the bag had been found, how much of the candy was consumed, and why I didn't take it away within seconds of discovering it.

I felt myself groping around for answers like a murder suspect. And from a cavern inside me the one answer I could give him rose up and touched the tip of my tongue, but would go no further. It's because I don't know what it's like to watch a two-year-old anticipate a wonderful surprise, I wanted to say, but there was no way to harness such strange thoughts and make them into a real sentence. It's because I don't know what a little boy like your little boy says when he's filled with delight! It was because I wanted to see...I so badly wanted to know, I needed to feel it, to have a moment of being a regular mom! This was my lonely defense. And it marked the essence of my isolation, but there were no words to describe it—then.

Over that night I fretted, and felt like a child myself, one who had been scolded into knowing she'd done something terribly wrong. But like the autumn clouds that day, everything blew over when it turned out the children were all right—even though my own personal storm was soon to begin. The little boy's dad and I never exchanged words after the telephone call, and a few months later, Charles and I took Will out of the preschool and enrolled him in a special school for kids with disabilities. I stayed on to help at Springbrook and fulfill my co-op agreement, however, even though I was certainly no longer obliged to. I continued my job as editor of the newsletter, brought in snacks, helped clean up the room. I watched over the three kids from the playground until June, as they grew and thrived and finished their year in the blue portable by the stream.

New Voice

"This is incredible," my voice teacher tells me, her brow knitted. "Maybe for now you should sit on the stool."

It's my first singing lesson in seven years or more. I stopped coming to this quaint house in the north part of Seattle, where my mentor makes little vocal miracles happen, before I got pregnant. Pregnancy and childbirth boldly ushered themselves into my unsuspecting life, and with all that came the bundle of a baby boy who required an unbelievable amount of attention as he grew and grew. No time for music, for my formerly pampered voice. Now I see some light as I emerge from the tunnel, and I feel like it's time to start working again. But I've pretty much lost it. Lost my vocal stamina.

Her expert hands grip my rib cage. "Breathe," she instructs. She sits back down at the piano. "Now: 'Team-o team-o team-o team-o team-o.'" A simple scale. "Team-o…team-o!" comes the squawk, and after that there's nothing left. The sound is pathetic, the tiny bleat of a newborn lamb. My serious and seasoned coach, who is also a dear friend, cannot contain herself. Suddenly we're both breaking up with laughter.

It's funny now, I guess, but I know how this amusing sound was formed. For one thing, I did not sleep for two years after Will was born. I danced. Danced him around the house at one a.m., two, three, since he never slept longer than a few hours at a stretch. All good singers are highly aware of the importance of rest. Then came the harder times, the crying times. Weeping can take its toll on the vocal cords, though I never knew it before. But now, in the voice studio, I can *feel* it.

After that came several years of intense speech therapy for my son. The whole family was involved. At age three, Will only had one or two words. The therapist told his father and me that we must talk to him all day long. We needed to loudly emphasize every word we uttered in his presence, and when he did come forth with a word, we were told we must repeat it, two, three times. We must read to him at every opportunity. Singing would be good too. These days followed the sleepless days and the crying days—these were the desperate days.

There was a window during which we must get our child to talk, or the window would quietly close and he might never have a voice. I threw myself into the program, of course. "Ka!" the golden-haired toddler would call. "Cat!" I replied. "Cat! Cat!" "Ba!" he cried out. "Book! Book!" All day long, day in, day out. I was automatically saying no to the recording studio jobs and the club dates that used to crowd my calendar. We could barely afford to have me pass up work, but there was a pressing situation at home that now demanded all my time—and my voice. I had a new career of crooning lullabies and nursery songs in addition to my job of talking all the time, and I performed it with more passion and commitment than I had ever poured into any previous gig. We visited a speech camp for boys with autism, for an appointment with the top speech therapist in Seattle. On our way into the office we passed the kids, average age ten, who were playing on the playground, hammering on chunks of wood, scrawling on the sidewalk with pieces of chalk. These kids were nonverbal. The tap-tap of the hammer was the only sound rising up out of the midst of seven or eight boys playing outside on a summer day. There was something magical and mysterious about it, seeing this bevy of special boys communicating on some other plane. A golden retriever rushed up to William. "Da!" said Will. There was hope.

In the back of my mind I had begun to prepare myself for a life of silence, the silence I had experienced among the boys at the camp. I researched the tools I'd seen them using that day, the sign language, the picture cards. We never put the cards into play, though, because there was a breakthrough. Just before he turned four, Will started to talk.

And that was when my own dreams, my other dreams, started to sail back to me, carried on the sweet notes of my son's new syllables, as the cage door flew open and he started chirping away at last like a wondrous baby bird.

I don't know quite how to explain this history to my teacher and friend, but I don't think I have to—the voice tells all, everything's there in my sad little squeak. You have to start all over again, the squeak tells me. You've given every ounce of vocal energy away to another cause, it croaks. You gave it up. Squawk, squeal. But you can get it back.

I return home from the lesson, run up our front walkway. "Where did you go, Mama?" Will is hanging out on the porch waiting for me. When he says "Mama" it always comes out in a French accent. "Where did you go?" He repeats most of his sentences. "I had a singing lesson!" I reply, clutching my practice tape in my hand. "I missed you Mama!" he says, little Frenchman, as he grabs my arm. " I missed you!"

It's a distant memory: I once regularly stood under hot lights, rhinestone earrings dangling, sequins twinkling, belting the tunes, stretching my arms out Judy Garland-style at the end where the big note comes. Now I am going to start all over again. I may even make a record when I'm ready. My dreams of musical glory have been renewed. I really believe in my heart that anything is possible.

Soul Deep

My dearest closest friend had just gotten the news that she was pregnant. And so her questions for me came rapid-fire over the telephone line—what did you eat, how much weight did you gain, did you do an amnio—all the things her new state of mind and body made her passionately curious about. How euphoric we both were that this time had finally arrived, how mad with glee, chattering excitedly about the new world we were going to share after years of an old friendship. But it was only the start of the interview and already something was beginning to break down, and I knew it had nothing to do with the telephone wires. Right in the middle of her inquiry there came an awkward pause—a space, the dropping of a word, just a momentary lapse. "You did have…well, you had your amnio, that's right…" The conversation was losing steam.

Though I might have been imagining it, it felt as if all of a sudden we both knew we shouldn't be discussing what I ate and what I did when I was pregnant. That maybe we should just change the subject, and later, without my knowing, she should turn to someone else with her important questions. One of us or both of us was aware in an instant that my pregnancy might not be the one she wanted to look to as an example, and we were already well into this talk before we realized it.

I know this silence, this space. It shows up sometimes when relatives or acquaintances are trying to express their sympathy that my child turned out differently than he might have. Toward the end of their heartfelt little speech there's this uncomfortable moment—is it mine or is it theirs?—and I feel it, and it passes, like something just blew through on a whispery breeze. It comes at the close of my monthly support-group meetings, a certain energy that is palpable, moving around the room; I can hear it though it has no sound, something reverberating in my bones. The social worker is trying to end the meeting, but several mothers are lingering at the table, not moving from their chairs, looking like they don't want to leave. Moments ago there was lively chatter: we may have discussed everything, feeding issues, attempts at discipline, insurance situations, and stress management. But we haven't talked about sorrow—we haven't talked about guilt. We haven't, and we probably never will, go to that place that is so silent and so deep, although it may be the most special, fragile thing we have in common with one another. And it doesn't really matter, for in a minute we can brush it away, change the energy, as chairs shuffle and car keys come out of purses and someone volunteers to bring the chocolate chip cookies for next month.

Perhaps we've all been advised by sources close to us: don't go there. I know that's what I was told right off the bat in the first week I was given the news about my two-and-a-half-year-old son. A few days after the diagnosis, Charles and I were sent by our pediatrician to an occupational therapist who was so sympathetic and sound that it seemed like a good idea to take her advice. "Are you experiencing a whirlwind?" she asked us when we brought Will in for his first visit, to a big room filled with balls and ramps and ropes hanging from the ceiling. "Yes," I answered, "and a certain amount of guilt." She was only the second professional of many we were to see on that first rocky ride through a series of clinics and we were ready to listen when she said, with a hand on my shoulder and great reassuring kindness: "Oh no, no…there will be no guilt."

I believed her for a second. In fact, I never had believed in that nasty word. I felt that life was full of surprises, that accidents could happen, and I tried never to place blame on anyone, especially myself. After we received news of Will's autism, everything seemed fairly close to all right as far as understanding my place in the whole complicated picture. I was caught up in a whirlwind—a whirlwind of reading, of researching, of networking with teachers and therapists and mothers, of focusing on my baby in a new way and frenziedly trying to meet his needs. I was so preoccupied I didn't have time to reflect. Besides, my research reassured me that autism could occur in children of parents from all walks of life, in children of healthy mothers, mothers of any age. Its origins were a complete mystery, and everyone agreed that no cause had been discovered. This knowledge was nicely in place in my head during the day, when the sun was bright and my baby's eyes were full of laughter and gaiety. Then night fell. While Will was tucked in his crib and darkness crept through the house, that feeling—just tiny pangs of it but pangs nevertheless—lingered at my bedroom door.

And there in the blackness, God only knows how many times I retraced the days of my pregnancy. I was positive I had gone scrupulously by the book. But if there had been a tiny slip here or there, now it stood out in my memory like the bold graphics on a road sign. The day I was raking the garden during my second trimester and I suddenly toppled over onto the lawn like Humpty Dumpty. I called my doctor, who told me everything was fine, that I didn't need to make an appointment. But should I have gone in to see her? It didn't seem like I'd taken that hard of a fall, but should I have done something more? And what about the time I was filling up my car with gas and a droplet of fuel spotted my maternity dress? I was on my way to a luncheon and I didn't have time to go back home and change my clothes. Fumes? Poison? Should mothers-to-be even be pumping their own gas?

And the controversy over early immunization. Only a few sources talked about it then; it was a rumor floating around a couple of websites. But I *had* made the choice to give my baby shots.

Should I have, should I have? Did I? How, why? The questions poured through my mind into the night, followed by fears about my family history—the alcoholism that lurked there, a developmentally delayed cousin I had rarely seen but whose face began to appear regularly in my half-dreams. There was a streak of anxiety running through my husband's side of the family—a relative had once mentioned it, and I began to ponder something I'd read about studies having found a history of anxiety in parents of children with autism. Unbeknownst to Will's father, I started letting him share in the guilt.

All these thoughts, all these emotions, as wild and unsubstantiated as they truly were, layered one upon the other. I fell asleep as a thousand tears fell on my pillow. I told a friend when it was all over that in these beginning days I had cried every night for six months. Why didn't you tell me, why didn't you call me? she begged. But this was a perilous and sinister cavern, guarded so heavily that no loved one would ever be allowed passage through its secret entrance.

Then, somehow, with the light of morning it was over. I was up with my little joyball of a toddler, running after him like any mom, the positive parent going to the wall for her kid. The days were filled with challenges, but what mother didn't have those? Nothing would stop me and very little could get me down. It was only in the silence of the dark when that feeling rolled forward like a wave and no matter what my rational mind tried to do to fend it off, in its power it would take me over.

I saw my counselor, who let me scream and pound the chair and empty out her Kleenex box. I read more, I talked with myself more, I began to see who I was again in darkness or day—Will's mother. I came to accept the magnitude of the mystery of it all. I lived with the monster and although it took awhile, at last I faced it, and in the end I faced it down.

I still know its power, though. And when it pops back around for a moment, I recognize it.

In the speech therapist's lobby the other day I met a young mother and her two sons—a five-year-old boy who had been diagnosed with autism, and his little brother, who was a typically developing toddler. She introduced them as such, and told me their names—Joe, the oldest and Josh, the tiny one. "I always say that Josh came into my life so that I didn't have to feel so guilty about having Joe," she confided, and once again, in the space that came after her remark, for that is the silence that follows me still, my stomach churned. I thought: Where does that leave me, then, and my only child who is so much the same as your Joe?

And so a few haunting pieces remain. I grapple with images in my head, of the women of the 1950s and '60s with children like mine who were called "icebox mothers" by the leading physicians of the time. In their utter innocence, they alone were held responsible for their child's inexplicable disorder and told by professionals to change whatever it was they were doing. So far from me, they weren't permitted the benefit of this society's enlightenment and progress, in the way a number of things are viewed: the disease of autism as well as the role of women and mothers. I can only wonder in awe—how long was the night, how devastating the isolation, for them? Their own doctors officially pronounced them guilty. I cannot imagine what kind of pronouncement came from their own hearts.

★ ★ ★

I now know a different kind of night. Somehow Will and I have fallen into this routine of lying together in the dark, singing songs and making up funny little jokes until it is time for me to give him a huge, tight hug, wish him sweet dreams, and kiss his cheek before leaving his room and letting him drift off to peaceful slumber. During the telephone discussion with my pregnant friend, I wish I could have found the golden seed of the first sentence to explain to her that this is what it is all about. That this is what her nine months of a healthy regime should yield: a mystery in the dark, a treasure that comes out of nowhere, someone whose warm, breathing skin you can hold so close, but someone for whom you cannot answer; your own child, a complicated, beautiful mystery. And every evening now, for a fleeting moment, I hold this sweet wonder close to my body in the quiet space of darkness, where once, before I really understood the gift that life can bring, I was so afraid to go.

Window

Once, I had a window on the world, or the world as it could be, if everything were perfect.

Will spent four years in a preschool and kindergarten designed for children with disabilities, part of a cutting-edge research center on the University of Washington campus. It was there that I think I may have received more training than any of the students. I learned how to be strong. I learned compassion. I learned that there is so much more to humanity than I could ever have imagined before it was necessary to enroll my child in this unique institution. A group of brilliant instructors, therapists, college students, psychiatrists, and little children appeared in my life all at once and let me know, each in their way, right off the bat: we know the meaning of the word hope, and the meaning of the word triumph. Let us show you. I was limping under a cloud of sadness at the time, but it really wasn't long before I broke through the fog and started running along their track of 100 percent positive energy.

The window—a room with one-way glass that allowed parents to view their kids at work and play in the classroom—was a daily part of my experience from the time Will and I first arrived at the school, known as the EEU (Experimental Education Unit). We had been incredibly lucky to find out about the place, which was rather a secret as it turned out—this was before the Internet, before such information for parents became available with the touch of the keyboard. Our doctor mentioned the initials (I immediately imagined a tiny university) during one of our appointments and when I called information to get the number, I found that the school was just four or five minutes away from our house. As soon as he was given an official diagnosis by a neurologist, Will was enrolled.

I remember walking through the portals of the school on the first day, holding the hand of my little son, as the raw breeze of early spring went through my fragile heart. I felt terribly resistant and deeply sad, to be somehow taking my child away from the "normal" world and walking him into a place for kids with serious problems. Yet in the same moment I felt blessedly safe. There were budding trees all around, and a green hill in the back of the school that rolled down to a shining blue waterway. There were hallways decorated with cheerful children's art, and a big play court with red and blue slides and bright green monkey bars, and sand tables and a dozen little tricycles lined up along a steel railing. At one end of the school was a small gym containing an assortment of physical and occupational therapy equipment—swings and ramps, even a mini- trapeze. There was a library for parents, with books you always thought would be for other people and not you, but now you leafed through them, you clung to them. There were meeting rooms, and a social worker's office. The school was quiet. It was a haven. If nothing else, we could hide here for awhile.

Part of the program at the EEU was to mix kids with challenges of all types—Down syndrome, autism, cerebral palsy, and some titles and labels I certainly had never heard of before—with typically developing, or "model" kids. So in fact we weren't hidden from the regular world—we were right in it. The two closest friends I made while there were moms of model kids. We watched our children with the same anticipation, we acknowledged each kid's achievements with the same high-five. The model parents saw how hard the special parents' lives were and tried to help, and the special parents realized that some of the things their child was going through were not at all different from kids' of any size or color or developmental level.

Will slid into the schedule with no trouble, and before I knew it there was a little bus honking at our door, there to whisk my three-year-old off to his busy day. The first year, his teacher was a soft-spoken young woman who understood the parents' anguish and led us gently into our new circle of friends. The second year, we had an athletic, outgoing blonde dynamo who challenged us on every level and who knew that Will was capable of much more than he sometimes showed. At every turn of the way Will was allowed to, and expected to, contribute and participate. Of course, these teachers had assistants—many assistants. There were college kids, male and female, students who adored the children, coming out of the woodwork. The principal strolled the halls, peeking into the rooms to see that everything was going according to plan. Children with behavioral challenges were not left out of the mix at the EEU. There were some explosive ones who screamed a lot, and others who occasionally needed to be wrestled to the ground. There was equipment to handle—helmets, wheelchairs, tubes. In spite of this, the classes traveled in groups on regular field trips where they experienced the real world. Most of the time it went without incident. There were inner city kids from low-income parents, and children from the surrounding upscale neighborhoods. It all happened on a level playing field, because there was no tuition at the EEU—it was free.

Will learned to read and write during these years, slowly and simply but miraculously, and he learned a little math. He learned to keep his balance on the playground and he learned to tolerate the feel of finger paint and sand and other textures—sensory integration therapy was a big part of his program. When he first came to the school, he didn't have whatever the thing is that motivates a kid to jump up and dance and sing when music starts to play, but a teacher would pull him up during circle time every day as the tunes rang out from the boombox, and soon he saw what it was all about. Mainly, he learned not to hide away, lost in spinning a toy on the floor. He held hands with other children. He looked into their eyes and said their names.

By Will's kindergarten year, our family was completely and utterly spoiled. We had become accustomed to regular roundtable meetings focusing on Will and only Will and everything Will was turning out to be and all he was going to need, with therapists, teachers, tutors, and

University of Washington honchos from the Department of Child Psychology in attendance. We had a support group and a newsletter featuring articles by mothers and fathers and all sorts of new information. All the parents received daily reports about their children, who were being constantly observed by professionals and by the young, enthusiastic students of the Special Ed teaching program. Better than anything, we could sit in the Observation Room ourselves and watch the class, and our children's progress, for as long as we wanted, often with a teacher joining us. We pretty much knew we had it made.

I was always bringing friends to the window room, knowing how it would blow them away. We'd sit back in our chairs, watching the typical kids help the others, seeing them laugh and sing together. We'd marvel at the challenged kids, who were often at their brilliant best during classroom time. One of my girlfriends was astounded as she brought her face closer to the glass. "You can't tell who's who!" she exclaimed.

My standard line as I escorted visitors down the hallway and back to their parking place under the trees was kind of a showing-off question: "When you look into that classroom, don't you see a perfect world?"

Then came the final ceremony, the break. Tiny kindergartners marched up to the podium in their paper graduation hats and received their diplomas. Some had to be led to the stage. One was pushed up in a wheelchair. One or two whirled around in a daze, tossed their diplomas into the air, and wandered toward the exit. When Will got up he looked out into the audience, proud as a peacock, searching for the faces of his mom and dad and aunt and grandmother who were sitting together and clapping wildly. A little song was played from a kiddie record: "We'll be together, together forever again."

The families went their separate ways, off into the land outside the green-leafed portals, the land that we all knew would have its tough side. Would we ever enjoy such attention, such understanding, or have the luxury of knowing our kids were way more than okay for a whole day again? The EEU even went to great lengths to place children in elementary schools with good programs and good special educators.

They did well by William, helping us to find the right "fit." But sometimes these days I'll run into an alumni mother in our local shopping center, or in a park. "I miss the window," we will both say.

And naturally we miss it. We were given a rare chance to watch our kids' lives unfold, as they grew by leaps and bounds, in what seemed to us to be a perfect world.

How the King Became the King[1]

There he sits on his little throne, Cheerios scattered on the table before him, and on the floor below. "I WANT JUICE!" he demands. "Can you say 'please'?" asks his lady-in-waiting—me. "PLEASE!" the shout comes back.

"Please" is how my son, a five-and-a-half-year-old monarch with an attitude, fools me into believing he has one iota of regard for me in this situation. I set the juice on the table. "JUNGLE CUP!" he cries angrily. Oops. Wrong move. Slave woman brought the juice in the bunny cup.

How did this happen? His preschool teacher warned me early on. "William exhibits a certain—*noncompliance* in the classroom," she reported. "If you let it go it'll be murder later on." Well. Now that Will is in kindergarten I'm wondering how "later on" got to be now, and what happened to my firm commitment to become a large-stick-carrying policewoman before things got out of hand.

I cut myself a small bit of slack actually, because even though I know that any loving parent can fall prey to the whims of his or her diminutive, sweet-cheeked dumpling, my situation may have been somewhat different. Waiting for Will to utter one word in the English language took such a painfully long time that I can almost pinpoint the moment in which I lost control and went the Way of the Wimp. There had been times when I thought he might never say "Mama."

Years had gone by during which I believed I'd always have to make every choice for him. His inability to express his preferences—pointing didn't seem to be a part of his repertoire—left him incredibly frustrated, and more so as he approached age three, three and a half. "Eh!" could mean "cookie" or "Eh!" could mean "bath," and the never-ending queries of people within earshot—"What did he say?"—tired me out. Though she tried nobly to interpret the one-syllable squeaks, even Mama, the eternal optimist, had to admit her heart was growing heavy.

Then one day, when he was almost four years old, Will and I were out for a drive together, stopped at a light. "Which way shall we go, Sweetie?" I chirped to the back seat. Before I could answer myself in the usual way and make the automatic turn in the direction of my choice, a high-pitched voice came back. "There!" it barked, and in the rearview mirror I looked up to see a grin of delight and a small finger pointing. I was stunned. I was dreaming. With my eyes wet and an enormous lump of gratitude in my throat, I made the left turn.

From then on his requests seemed like big miracles, and my desire to reinforce them knew no bounds. Cookies? Yes, yes, here's a whole box! Playground? Yes, darling, we can stay for the whole day! McDonald's?? You can pronounce McDonald's? *McDonald's* you say! And, with an attack of giddiness, I would set my car in the direction of the legendary rainforest-killer.

A dynamo was emerging and right off the bat he had a willing follower. With his newfound power Will became more settled, more cheerful, and even teachers and speech pathologists became victims of his charm. I wasn't the only one. But somehow, for the others, he learned how to be courteous most of the time. He was saving up the outrageous stuff for behind closed doors.

I don't want to give the impression that his father and I haven't set limits. We know it would be wrong to send him out into the world thinking he can squawk orders and mountains will move. Almost every day now we find it necessary to enforce a "Time Out" or two. We don't throw tantrums in the department store. We don't use the neighbor's daffodils as a trampoline. We don't hit our parents in the face.

But taking a stand on unacceptable behavior is one thing. Dealing with this concept that someone forty-eight and a half inches tall controls the entire Western Hemisphere is another. And every now and then when he finds it deep down within himself to say "I love you, Mama," his status, already too high in our household, somehow moves a notch higher.

The Greek chorus echoes in my ears. "You'll pay for it," said Madame Psychic the preschool teacher. "You'll pay for it," said my best friends, who also happen to be supermoms. I'm paying for it. But it can't go on. We can't have a dictatorship around here, it just won't work, I'm going to have to crack down, I shall have to get mean, I must consult my child-rearing books, attend a parenting class. Meanwhile, there he sits on his little throne, and though his pounding fists shake the table he himself seems unshakable.

"I WANT RAISINS! PLEASE!"

He throws his head back with glee, his eyes twinkling, his giggles so infectious they melt my heart. The king can talk. The king can express himself beautifully. The king is alive and well and confident and happy. Here come the raisins. Long live the king.

Note

1   This essay was originally published in *The EEU Connection*, Spring 1997.

I Can't Explain It

I've passed this homeless guy before. Panhandling on the corner of a bustling downtown street, barely protected from the cold concrete by a tattered sleeping bag and some dirty blankets, he makes loud conversation and collects coins in his coffee tin from the people hurrying by. Whenever I've come near him in the past he's shouted out to me, not to ask for anything but just to say hello—he's crusty and hardened, of course, but he's also a sweet, sandy-moustached old geezer who likes to draw attention to himself. "How's it going today?" he'll say to me in a voice crackly from an ancient cough.

Normally I smile and nod in brief but friendly fashion, but normally I'm by myself. Today I have William with me, and as is always the case when we come close to anybody who might throw us a cheerful greeting, I must approach with caution. An unexpected hello from anyone, friend or stranger, could cause Will to explode into a spectacular tantrum, make him dart headlong into oncoming traffic.

Hand in hand, my little boy and I have to walk past the gentleman to get to where our car is parked. Now my antennae tell me there is danger. Instead of a quarter, this afternoon some passerby has apparently handed the guy a sky-blue balloon. As he spots us coming toward him, he seems to be getting ready to hand it to Will. I know that if he makes even so much as a gesture in our direction—especially with this bright, looming prop—there'll be screaming and struggling from Will and we'll cause a scene. But I have a routine; I've become expert at getting out of these things. Just as we pass the fellow and he's saying "Here you go little one!" and the unwanted balloon is floating in our direction, I grab Will's arm to move him quickly toward the car. "Let's go, Will," I say sharply, and over my shoulder with an apologetic glance I call out to the man: "I can't explain it!"

It's my pat cry. It has taken a number of practice sessions and some tough public experience to get the phrase programmed into the computer but now it's there, ready in a click, a little scrap of armor I can use to fend off looks, stares, commentary, or, in this case, a string of expletives as the old gentleman's sweetness turns street-sour. "What?" hollers the guy. "You think I'll contaminate him? Don't want him to come near me? Why you..." and the trail of obscene names he has chosen to describe this uptight overprotective mother trail off into the city air as my son and I make our escape.

Just like my kid's, my instincts have taught me to flee. In the moment of flight, however, I always feel a desperate need to plead my case. If there were time—if there would ever be time after we've run into a classmate of Will's in the park by surprise, for instance, or seen an adored former teacher in the grocery store—I would love to sit down and explain everything I know. I would tell everyone that even though this little person is reacting negatively, it is really the exact opposite of what he wants—truly, he would be thrilled to take a bright blue balloon; he would love to stay and talk with a friend. But one of the characteristics of his unique persona is that he simply can't handle something he didn't expect, didn't know was coming. He wants, craves, and needs predictability. On the afternoon we encountered the old man and the balloon, I would have had to set up a special meeting with the street gent. I'd have needed to get an exact description of the size and color of the balloon, figure out the names of the streets where we would meet, tell the guy what to say and how to hand over the toy, go home and draw some kind of picture and write a story of what was going to happen and how, and, finally, present the story to Will. Even then there would be no knowing how Will would react.

So, yes, I'll tell you all about it if I have the opportunity and the time. And I will go to those lengths, setting up meetings and writing stories—it's a technique I learned a few years ago, and I have used it many times with positive results. But if traffic is whizzing by and Will is on the run and a balloon is looming like a scary ascending monster, I'll have to toss you my well-rehearsed line and run, no matter what you may think of me. And though I may seem angry or upset or a little crazy, I really am, for a moment, only sad. Sad that we can't meet and greet and tip our hats to you as anyone else would be perfectly happy to do under the circumstances.

When Will was an infant, long before I found out he had autism, I would use this same phrase in earnest. I really couldn't explain it: why I couldn't pop him in the car seat and go visit a friend for an afternoon because I knew there would be wailing at every "unexpected" stoplight; why he turned and crawled away when a cute cuddly toy was offered; why a sudden change in direction in the car or even the stroller would upset him to the point of baby hysteria; why he wouldn't touch even a sugar-coated cereal treat or a cookie. ("Offer it to him differently," my friends would suggest. "Put it in a different dish!") And these well-meaning friends—mothers, all of them—could not stop asking questions, giving advice. Maybe if you don't cater to him so much. Maybe he's too insulated, maybe he needs to be in daycare with other children. A grandmotherly figure in his life thought that he might be a genius. When I talked to myself, this was the explanation I chose.

Then at last, when he was singled out by the teacher at his first school, we took him to be diagnosed. I thought I'd get a big document from the brain doctor that I could edit down and use on friends, relatives, everyone who had seemed perplexed by his early behavior. But there was no document. It turned out that his condition was so mysterious that, although studies had been done and strides had been made, little had been discovered so far. Basically, no one knew very much. With whatever information I could gather, I was going to have to write my own script.

And so it happened that as Will's dad and I found ourselves more and more in situations where our son became afraid and out of control in public, I was forced to develop my first speech for the world to hear:

"It's autism rearing its ugly head again!" I would recite it with a weary, slightly bitter chuckle when Will fought and flailed in supermarkets, parking lots, hospitals, shopping malls, and in the middle of the sidewalks of our city. As I straddled this tiny tot lying face down on the cement, both of us exposed to the curious or shocked expressions of passersby, someone might ask me what was wrong and I'd look up with a nutty grin, perspiring from wrestling the force of fifty pounds, fighting back tears and hoping that somehow the blunt truth would make it perfectly clear to one and all: "It's autism...rearing its ugly head...!"

But the A-word rarely managed to get me the attention and assistance I needed. Once a doctor stopped to help, and occasionally a security guard would hustle over and kindly lift Will to a place where he could get himself organized and begin again—after the guard had determined the boy wasn't being beaten. But usually people just glanced at us and rushed past, leaving me with my emotions and the daunting job of trying to calm, calm, calm this hysterical child. My last, pathetic attempt at getting strangers to understand us came during lunch hour on a crowded avenue, after Will had become terrified by some random sight or sound. I was fighting him to the ground to prevent him from running in front of a bus that was barreling down the boulevard. In the blur of activity, I heard a man shout, "Hey lady, stop beating on your kid!" Startled, I braced Will and looked up through the crowd to find whoever had said it. "It's autism..." I whimpered to no one, to everyone, as tears streamed down my cheeks and people brushed past us. A woman came over and tapped my shoulder hard. "It's child abuse!" she barked and walked away.

That incident helped to cure me, liberate me. I really no longer cared what people thought. I needed a quick signal, something that would whisk me past the potential judgment like the horn of an engine that speeds through a clanging railroad crossing. Furthermore, I was certain Will didn't need to hear such a stark description of his actions, didn't need to hear that label again, didn't need to be labeled, really—by now I absolutely hated that label. As long as I was going to have to face these situations and get out of them in a hurry, I figured that I might as well wrap my feelings up in a neat little package and go ahead and blurt them out, I would yell them out, scream them out in as brief a moment as possible. I would find a way to say it all without really saying it: It's one of the most hideous disorders a person can have!! Sometimes it's almost impossible to deal with! It has moments when it can't be controlled! But he's really a wonderful child, the sweetest most loving kid there is and we have found our way through everything to make a very happy family!

And now that's the message concealed beneath the surface of my one-sentence shout. My little boy wants a balloon like any other little boy. My little boy loves attention and loves new people and wants to be around them. But here he is, hollering away, struggling in my arms with all the energy of a lightning bolt. I can't explain it.

Desiree

"Everything carries better in a pack." Will is looking out the living room window, gazing out onto the twin maple trees in our front yard.

"Yes, dear."

"Four new tires, one hundred dollars."

"Yes honey."

"Natural Foods."

"Mmm-hmm."

"'No phony lures'—the one with the fish! Those were the signs!" He's giddy, taking himself on a trip down memory lane.

Yes, yes, those were the signs. Or the slogans, on a billboard around the corner from our house, at the intersection where shady neighborhood lanes stream onto a bustling boulevard. Will remembers every line from every ad that went up during the years 1994 through 1996. That was when I had to start reading them to him, though they seemed to send him such a strong message back then that for all I know he may have been reading them himself.

"Weisfield's Jeweler's!" he reminisces. "Do you remember I was afraid of the signs?" Giggles erupt from him. He gets down on the floor and starts to roll around.

Do I remember? I remember it was not at all funny, standing in front of the parenting section in Barnes and Noble wondering where on the shelf existed the self-help tome that was going to get me out of this one.

He was but a one-year-old when it started to happen.

So many times when we were out driving and we rounded the corner toward home, Will would let out a frightened cry. I always thought it was because he didn't want to go back to our house, that he just wanted to keep driving, driving, as he seemed to love to do. When he turned three, the cry changed to "Na! Na!"—at the same place, the same stoplight every time, with me hopelessly straining in the rearview mirror to try to figure out the expression on his face. Then at four he could talk, and he clued me in. "Don't go past the sign!" he wailed. "Don't go past the sign!"

Oh my god. It was so obvious, yet I'd never seen it. This great big bold thing ascending over us on the corner, with letters thirty feet high. But what was the problem? It had a picture of a giant watch on it right now. Awhile back it had the face of a cute doggie, and before that some radio station's call letters....

And then the light bulb flashed on, after years of worry and bafflement and reaching my hand into the back seat to hold his little arm. Every six weeks or so, the billboard would change. There would be a new ad, a different picture, a logo we couldn't see coming. The sign. He wasn't able to predict what the sign was going to be, and at a certain time every month he would get scared, knowing times and dates as he inexplicably does, and knowing the sign was going to change on him.

It was the first of July, and as usual his calendar sense was dead-on. The billboard was going to change any day, I knew—I'd been watching it closely now, estimating, calculating, feeling like a Vegas bookie. Our route was going to take us underneath it. William stood in the doorway, legs steadfast, blond curls shaking in the summer sun. "No go in car," he mumbled in a tiny voice. But we had to go. We had to get over this one; we had to find a way. Although there was another road we could take, this whole thing had been jangling our nerves, both his and mine, for too long.

I tried cookie bribes and M&M bribes even though these measures had no track record of ever working for me. "Do you want me to call The Sign Lady?" I sighed at last, and it came out of nowhere. There wasn't a sign lady that I knew of—this is what mothers naturally do, they make up SuperFairies to make the scary spider go away. But it quickly came to me that if there was a Sign Lady, a goddess of billboards, then I wanted her. I *needed* her. I remembered the name Ackerman from the bottom of the board—of course I remembered every detail of that board, having scrutinized it out of desperation for so many years. I grabbed the Yellow Pages. I found the phone number. What was I going to ask? That a crew come over now and take the whole thing down ASAP? I dialed. "Ackerman, this is Desiree!" chirped a happy voice on the end of the line. I launched into a fast rap that came from a deep place of insanity and carried me along a swift current to another deep place of insanity, knowing all the while that Desiree would think I was a crank caller.

"Oh hi Desiree I know this is going to sound really crazy but my son and I drive past one of your billboard signs almost every day, the one at the corner of Union Bay Place? And he's just little and he has some special challenges and he—he…" I looked over at the door where Will was still standing, frozen like a baby deer, with enormous eyes fixed upon me. "Yes?" Desiree urged. She was actually listening to me. Suddenly it felt like I had my beloved family doctor on the phone as I described the onset of symptoms no legitimate physician had ever heard of. "…we would like some information! We wondered if you can tell us when the sign is going to change. My little boy gets frightened when it changes. We want to know what's going to—well, I mean, what we need to know is—well, what's going to be on it next!" It was confirmed: I was a bona fide nutcase. But Desiree hadn't hung up.

"Oh my goodness…okay," said the sign goddess slowly as she tried to process my inquiry. "I think I understand. We, um, we don't mind giving you that information. Let's see, ah, I'll check my book. Hold on for a minute." This gal might be considered a dependable customer service rep by some but by the time she came back to the phone I knew she was a glorious angel sprouting wings. There was a billboard fairy. I was going to get my kid into the car again.

"This current one is going to change on July fifth," she prophesied. "It will go from the picture of the watch to an ad for a coffee drink with a photo of a cup and big black letters on a red background. Is that what you need to know?" I repeated all this for Will as she was talking. "July fifth…coffee…black letters…" and I wanted a videocam to record his body language as he relaxed, relaxed, relaxed. Where will he take me next, I thought, as I went with him into a blissed-out state. Here we are backstage of the sign rental biz. Yes, this was what we needed to know.

And on that day we got into the car with a new lease on life. Desiree had given Will a fantastic gift—a picture. A picture in his mind of what was coming around that frightening bend in the road. The Rolex would be there for three or four more days and then the new background would be up in all its crimson glory. He still gripped the sides of his car seat in nervous anticipation as we approached the coffee ad. But things gradually got better and better. At the beginning of each month as we got ready to go somewhere, Will would say "Call Desiree?" It was after a few more predictions from her crystal ball that he started to commit the slogans of the ads to memory, and print them out on his white board at home, and even enjoy them, and laugh at the funny ones.

By autumn, Des and I were staunch comrades.

She had interpreted my craziness for what it was—a cry for help. For a moment once a month, her desk job became part of the helping profession. "Oh it's you, Kelly, I knew it!" she would say when I called. "How is Will doing?" He was doing so well that eventually, after eight or nine months, I didn't have to call anymore.

These days he grins at the memory of it. And I recall that time with the same gratitude in my marrow. Oh Des, Des, where are you now? Are you CEO of the Ackerman Billboard Company? Did they give you the promotion you deserved? You'll never know how you saved us. You got us through. You were the Sign Lady.

School Picture

The principal of Will's preschool called me on the phone. "The class photos have come in!" she almost shouted into my answering machine. "You won't believe William! He's grinning, he's looking right into the camera—he looks like an angel!"

This was unusual, the principal actually calling our house. But there was a reason for it. Anyone who knew Will knew that getting a decent "formal" photo of him was something to get excited about, and when I played back the message, I felt a sensation which at the time was just beginning to become familiar to me (whereas months down the line it turned into a part of me, my way of being, my M.O.). My heart would race with excitement over some possible positive development, then hold back and hold on, because in fact in the end the news might not live up to the expectations of a mother whose emotional state hung on whatever the report might be. The heart galloping ahead, then holding its breath, starting, stopping.

But when the picture came home in Will's Barney backpack, it indeed was a prizewinner. The top of his little mop of curly hair shone white-gold in the studio lights. His cheeks were peachy-pink. He was grinning directly into the camera, and the whole effect was angelic. Any parent would have remarked, were it their little sweetheart—gosh, what a great school photo! But for me it was more than that. My spirit now had permission to soar. This was my son—stuck on a stool where normally he'd have wriggled like a puppy, facing a strange photographer which was certainly, for him, a promise of torture—captured in a flash at his best. Calm, smiling out at the world, confident and happy—this was a Kodacolor miracle.

Gazing at this picture reminded me how far we'd come from Will's first try at modeling, which took place the year before, in a "normal" preschool classroom, when I had no idea anything was up with Will, before the pediatrician had delivered the stunning news that there were some serious and profound problems affecting my child. At that photo session, both Will and I were frantic, operating at the absolute edge. The teacher at the school had warned the parents that it would be no picnic to organize this group shot, that there was going to be chaos and crying for sure. But as moms and dads took the hands of wee ones and herded them over to the blue mark on the floor, my kid took off for the exit, shouting hysterically. He pounded and kicked and wailed against the wobbly door as I tried to reassure him, attempted to restrain him, moved to shield my beet-red face from the other parents. There was no way, as there had been no way in many situations before this, to stop him from breaking away. We ran off into the wet February night together.

In those very early days, we were often beating a retreat, in a panic, on the run, tears stinging our faces. Weeks then passed, and we received a copy of the group shot in the mail. The bright assortment of kiddie faces had come together all in a row after we'd slammed the door and left. Each tiny countenance glowed, as cute as a little bug. Here was printed evidence to show that when it came to connecting with others, Will was an outlaw: he does not appear in his first class picture. I showed it to him, and when he saw it he moved his hand over the photograph. "Eh," he said, and I knew what he was trying to say—"School."

Now years have gone by and I still stare with pride and relief and wonder at Will, age three and shining, in his first school picture, standing in a frame at his parents' bedside. This in all the world must be my favorite image. It bears no hint of the struggles leading up to the moment it was frozen in time: no sign of the day his mom, two teachers, and two therapists had to move his toddler's body inch by inch into the school, across a whole parking lot, down a long corridor, and slowly, with much pain all around, into his classroom (because of some terrible mysterious fear that had gripped him and because he could resist with such astonishing strength). It can't show the terror he could and still does experience when a loud, unexpected sound comes out of the blue, and it doesn't give away the secret that, even at three years old, he was speaking only in vowel sounds. Nor does it warn of the challenges to come—walking into a public elementary school classroom, learning to fasten the snaps on a jacket, trying with enormous concentration and frustration to understand the quick pace of a cartoon video, and still needing to summon his courage every time he has to hold his expression in front of the daunting camera light.

This photograph displays my son in one of his great moments, as he beamingly hands over with innocence and ease the kind of gift that, at one time or another, every mother may be privileged to get from her kid. And in that moment, the only thing the mother can see is all future, all joy.

One Dream

Grandma

When Will's first two-syllable word came, it was "Grandma."

I was the only one who heard it. We were leaving my mother-in-law Charlotte's house the day after Thanksgiving and I leaned down to button Will's jacket as he stood in the hallway. I said, "We're going to say goodbye to Grandma now." He answered as clearly, cleanly, and crisply as a little English professor (after years of calling her "Ga"): "Grandma!"

This might have been my first clue that a relationship made in heaven was about to get started. It made perfect sense that Will would try to reach out to his beloved Gram. Grandma saw plainly all of Will's difficulties—in communicating, in trying to be with people, even in attempting to sit for a few moments at her table for holiday dinners. Grandma, veteran of the child-rearing wars, could see that Will was very different from any other child she'd had experience with. But Grandma didn't care.

I once found a section entitled "Autism" in the medical encyclopedia that sat on her table near the fireplace (she had enjoyed a long career as a nurse). "Here it is, Mom," I said. "Here are three or four pages about it."

Charlotte glanced over the section for a moment. "Interesting," she said. She never tried to deny Will's illness—I had already talked her ear off on the subject, and, with her keen intelligence, she had soaked up quite a bit of knowledge. But she thought for a moment.

"You know, with two highly sensitive artists for parents," she began, "it follows that he would be as sensitive as he is—doesn't it?"

Who was I to argue? It was simpler for her, and she didn't need any fancy diagnostic terms. She grew up in Ohio, in a big old-fashioned painting of a farmhouse with a huge front porch, and an outhouse and pigs that were butchered every season and chickens she and her sisters would chase after. She learned the piano, a talent she had kept using all her life. She went to nursing school and found her career. She met the man of her dreams and they managed to bring up five beautiful kids. They moved out to a gorgeous hunk of wilderness in the Northwest and built their home and there they remained. Life was pretty straight ahead. She is of a certain solid Midwest mentality that her modern-day citified West Coast daughter-in-law just sits and marvels at.

So that is how she prefers to think of William, as her sensitive grandson. And she knows him well. I've seen the two of them walking in the woods that border her log-cabin house. I've seen Will lying lazily in her arms, rocking in the antique chair on her deck in the autumn sun. Not many words pass between them. But when Will is in the vicinity of his grandmother, she showers him with her serenity and her good cheer, and all is right in their world.

He would have had another grandmother, my mother. But my mom died three years before Will was born. I wonder what Kaye would have thought of him, how she would have reacted to him. She had a hard time facing life's tricky realities and she often could face them only after having swiftly downed a few stiff cocktails. She liked to be able to say things were better than they were. In my elementary school years she had picked up and left me, her only child, on a couple of occasions, leaving my dad and me to search for her, sometimes driving hundreds of miles together in the car. She would disappear for weeks at a time without any warning, and my father would sniff around her workplace and her friends, asking questions and looking for clues.

Later I learned from my mother that she had run off with other men, and that her dependence on alcohol, which she battled all her life, had played a part too. I think that from time to time and apartment to apartment she got tired of dealing with me and with her hard life as a waitress married to a bartender. But the bartender was committed to their marriage and relentless in trying to track her down, and when I was eight she returned to the nest for good, vowing never to leave, and thank God it was not too late to repair the damage. We slowly grew close, though we were as opposite as opposite could be. I was quiet and shy like my father. Kaye was feisty, willful, always laughing and charming the pants off anyone who came in contact with her. She was buddies with everyone.

When my mother came home at last, she proved to me over and over again that her love had no boundaries, that I was the center of her universe. But as I entered my teen years, she denied things about me. She couldn't accept that I was not popular in school, not the pretty thing she had been as a young girl. She wanted me to be some model of teenage beauty and loveableness, and I never was there, so I did my best to entertain her with song and dance. This is what comes back to me when I imagine what she might have been like as a grandmother to William. She would have loved him, with the power of the moon and the stars, for that was how her strong, beautiful heart was made, but she would have denied his disease, or sat late into the night with a glass of red wine wondering how she could fix it. Or maybe not.

No one who met Kathleen Bartley Williams ever forgot her. When she died in my arms at age sixty-seven (of a number of causes that I just say add up to "too much life"), neither of us would ever have believed that I was one day going to become the mother of someone myself. Neither would the jillions of people who came to her memorial service, since it was always my "career" she was touting to everyone within earshot, even when the career was flagging in the dust. But now I've brought the boy who would have been her only grandchild into the world, and sometimes I believe it is her descended-from-Irish blood alone that gives me what it takes to cope. In the meantime Kaye, the funster, plays her little joke on me daily. When William gets a mischievous idea in his head, his eyebrow goes up and his upper lip curls in the most enchanting little smile, and he flashes me a look, and though I am the only one who really recognizes it, there is my mother—Will's other Grandma. With the light of her determination in his eye.

So now, with both the granddads gone for years, Grandma Charlotte is the one living grandparent Will has.

★ ★ ★

One day at her house, Will allowed his grandmother to sit down at the piano and show off her marvelous style. This is the kind of moment that can go either way—the "surprise" of it can, of course, turn Will inside out and make him start hollering for everything to stop. But I think it was the way she slid gently onto the piano bench and tinkled the keys a little to warm up, and asked him softly if it was all right for her to play. She shuffled through her music books and found the song: "Look to the Rainbow" from *Finian's Rainbow*, and as she followed the notes, the melody chimed through the house. In an instant, Will fell quiet, uncharacteristically frozen in a trance. And from that charmed minute on, his grandmother could never get out of performing for him—he asks her to play that song on every holiday, at every visit. Grandma slips into place on the piano bench, her fine silver hair done up in a French twist and her apron still on from the earlier basting of the turkey. In her mid-seventies now, she is still statuesque, elegant-looking, an accomplished musician. There's a big leather chair next to the upright and Will jumps into his seat a few inches from the keyboard. Then the magic of her music fills the air.

With the fire crackling in the big brick fireplace and the lamps turned low, after the clatter of dishes in the kitchen has died down, toward the end of each family holiday now there is a tradition.

"Well, Will, what's your favorite?" Grandma asks.

"Look to the Rainbow!" Will chirps.

And his aunts and uncles gather around. I feel the presence of my own music-loving mother in the room. There's a sweet introduction played by weathered hands to a perfectly captive little boy, and Grandma sings softly all the way to the last refrain:

"Look, look, look to the rainbow

Follow the fellow who follows a dream

Follow the fellow

Follow the fellow

Follow the fellow who follows a dream."

A Boy Named Colin

The boy came up to his chair at the front of the conference room. He was a tall, lanky teenager, in a white shirt and black pants, and wearing glasses. His mother, an attractive forty-ish woman with swept-up hair and a big smile, brought him a mug of water and took a seat near him in the front row. A hush came over the room.

The support group was gathered on a Tuesday evening as usual, but tonight the room was packed with fifty or more folks, as many parents as I had ever seen there. I had come alone, while Charles watched Will. Everyone involved with this group for parents of kids with autism or Asperger's syndrome had sent a rep, for we had all received a mailer informing us: tonight was the night Colin would speak.

Colin was beginning to be famous in the community. He was in demand as a speaker now, having done a couple of conventions, even one out of town, for the Autism Society. We were probably lucky to get him. And once in his presence we felt more than lucky. We'd spent most of our parenting lives trying to unravel a mystery, piece by piece, moment by moment, one little tug-of-the-heart at a time. Here, in this nondescript hospital meeting room with fluorescent lights over our heads, we wondered nervously if we could find another puzzle piece. We were all here, quiet, waiting. You could hear people's thoughts, really: Is this who my child might turn out to be?

He had no papers, no notes. He sat back in his chair, looking only slightly nervous, and began to talk to us as if we were friends. "My name is Colin," he announced. "I'm seventeen and I go to Fairview High. I'm here to tell you a little bit about myself and about my Asperger's syndrome."

Immediately we were stunned. This handsome, sandy-haired guy could have been a talking head on your evening news. He made perfect eye contact with the audience, his speech was clear as a bell, and within seconds he seemed to warm up to the crowd. His fingers fidgeted a little, and that was all.

He began by going through the story of his school life. And now we did see a trace of the rigidity that would automatically be a major part of his autism spectrum disorder, the intense need for structure his audience was all too familiar with. He was clinging to chronological order. "In first grade—I had some trouble fitting in. In second grade—I moved to another school. In third grade…" His story outline provided him with a way to talk to us. But his mother chimed in from her seat nearby. "In other words, elementary school was hell," she told us all. Colin laughed. It was wonderfully obvious in the very opening of his forty-five minute lecture that Mom was his sidekick.

Finding the right education for Colin had been a rough road, according to his story and the additional comments his mother made. A number of schools didn't work out. He had the problems of a child with Asperger's syndrome: social deficits that stood in the way of everything. Some processing problems. A need for sameness, for predictability. Now, sitting here, he was able to recount it in his own words. It was amazing.

With much outside therapy he had made it to high school, where he had a couple of friends. They were computer nerds, and mostly they sat side by side, trading off at the screen playing games. He was on the computer every spare minute of his day. He called the "normal" people of the world "NTs"—neurotypicals. The other kids at school, the ones who looked at him curiously—they were all just "NTs." When Colin told us this, we burst into laughter. He grinned, and you knew he was getting into this new life as lecture-circuit jokester for autism.

Then there was a moment when his Asperger's syndrome actually did take over. Colin told us of how he had had to change high schools the previous year. Apparently the old school could not meet his needs. It didn't provide a place for him to "pace" between classes, one of the ways he regrouped during the day, as well as some other accommodations he didn't mention because by the time he was telling this part of his story, tears were rolling down his face, fogging up his glasses. He was trying to explain the difficulty of changing from one school to the other, how he had been put on a new bus route. That devil—change. He tried to talk about it but couldn't finish. In the middle of the miracle of this boy giving a speech to grown-ups, here was something I recognized from my own life with a boy like Colin. He wept, he ached, just thinking about a disruption in his routine. He froze. The room fell completely silent and someone handed Colin a Kleenex. No one knew what would come next, but since we were all used to scooping up our kids and flying out the door on a second's notice and bringing everything to a stop, we were prepared for whatever the next moment might be.

But it was not the end of the story. After a few minutes he worked his way back and carried on as if nothing had happened. He was on a "medication cocktail" he told us, four different drugs that were the result of much experimentation by the leading docs in Seattle. He listened to classical music all the time on his Discman. "Girlfriends?" he repeated, after someone in the audience got up the nerve to ask the thing that in the final question-and-answer period of the meeting lapped at the edge of all our minds. "I do talk to girls sometimes. I just seem to be too busy with my computers. Girls aren't that interesting to me, and I don't think I would be someone who would be that interesting to them." That was it—move on. He really was, I sensed, dying to talk about his computer games. Dying to take us to the brink of boredom with each and every detail about how each and every moment of each and every game transpired. Another trait I would've recognized right away.

I came to the meeting carrying so much stuff with me, and it wasn't in my purse. I brought the hours and hours of worry I'd known, eyeing teenagers on the street or in the mall, with their gangs, their attitudes, their sheer power. I brought all the time I'd put in looking at television, seeing movies, wondering with every single viewing whether my own son, with his sensory-processing difficulties, would ever be able to enjoy such light and sound. I brought gossamer dreams that my kid, a guy with a resistance to all things new, might someday eat pizza or attend a baseball game. I brought the echoes in my head of words Will had uttered in his cheerful innocence: "After college I will probably get married!" I looked at this boy, Colin—no, I didn't look at him, I scrutinized him down to the button on his buttoned-down collar—in the hope of seeing what Will's future would be.

And I was not alone. During the question period everyone had hung breathlessly on every answer. Colin and his mother, several times during his talk, performed the most wonderful duet. "The clothes you see here," he said when someone asked about wardrobe, "are the clothes I wear every day—a white shirt and black jeans." "He's not kidding," she followed. "We have a dozen white shirts and eight pair of black jeans. Easy shopping." She winked at him.

This teenager had triumphed. He was absolutely charming, in his different way. He was unbelievably articulate—he was doing well. The mom and her laugh and her wink, right there in an instant, may have had something to do with all this.

He got up and said goodnight with a yawn and no emotion, having floored us all. A number of parents moved in to get Mom's phone number and email. Colin may have helped some of us dump a few things from our bags full of worries in the conference room that night. All I know is that for some reason I walked out of there feeling remarkably light—an NT on Cloud Nine.

Lighting the Candles

Christmas morning, five a.m. I peek in at Will. He is sprawled out in the dark in his bed, arms and legs akimbo, face pale and peaceful, beautiful full lips still as the moon. There is no hint of the tyrant he has lately been discovered to be, the strutting little boss of our home. In sleep he's a miracle, all innocence and calm.

How hard it is to believe, looking at him in this pose, that only a day or so ago he was lunging at lamps, banging his fists against a table, creating a terrible scene, making his anger loudly known for all the neighbors to hear. I caused it to happen. I tied one sparkling red and green holiday ribbon around the neck of one of our living room lamps. It was too much for him. All the stuff of Christmas—as any parent knows—all adds up to too much stuff. For a kid who is pro-grammed with different software, it can be much worse. Last night, on Christmas Eve, he fell asleep thinking dreamily of Santa, but the week preceding his sugarplum dreams was a nightmare.

I tried to gently introduce the tiny decoration. I sat Will down on the couch. "William," I told him, "ever since you were a baby boy, we've had Christmas decorations." We have hung sparkly things in the past. But somewhere in the last few years Will blew the whistle on it all. "We always put a few ribbons here and there"—I pointed to the exact places I was thinking of hanging them up—"and we always set out the wonderful Christmas cards people send us—all our good friends!—right over there." I point, to the exact, exact place. I thought

I was expert at this kind of preparation since I've had an amazing amount of practice at it. I would keep talking and keep pointing for a few days, and then I would whip out the ribbons and the cards.

But no. A few days later Will entered the room and within a fraction of a millisecond he saw the decorations. "No! No no no no!" As I ran around to lamp and tables trying to save my little works of art, he became more agitated as he began pulling down ribbons and cards, and at last I knew the best thing was to simply give it all up. Give up, once again, something that is so important to me and in a quick moment so reprehensible to him, or at least something he feels a desperate urge to take power over.

Everyone has their dream of Christmas, and I'm aware that anyone who has a child living in their home may face a possible meltdown amidst the music and cheer and Santa hysteria. But my fantasy of the holidays never included a wee one knocking over furniture and tearing things off walls. I do have to admit that the choir of caroling angels answered my prayers on a couple of counts—Will loves the idea of Santa, and he adores the Christmas tree. In spite of how he may feel about other stuff being hung around our home, he is enchanted by each and every ornament that twinkles from the tree's fragrant branches. Because it's an unchanging ritual, he has accepted with joy our yearly trip to the tree nursery, and from the time the noble fir arrives in our living room, spends all his time looking at it and fingering the stars and hearts and brilliant balls. From the beginning I sensed that I should be grateful for this surprising gift of Will's delight. And now that the tree is the only holiday item that doesn't hold potential for an explosion (why, I continually wonder), I cherish its presence. I bow to it and consider it holy. Since tradition always looks the same, there are some traditions our family automatically can expect to maintain.

Yet I wish I could tie those ribbons. I long to paint snowflakes in the window. I feel a need to light candles every evening during Christmastide, and to keep a fire blazing in the fireplace. Why can't I? After exhausting every positive parenting technique, how can you sit down with a child and in a stern voice try to reinforce the appropriate behavior? How do you attempt to strictly discipline him around a picture of a cuddly white bear in a red Santa hat on the front of a Christmas card?

I am very capable, like a high-strung kid myself, of going off and whining and sobbing over this thing that is getting in the way of my holiday fun. But luckily I am the mother and not the kid, and, as Christmases have come and gone, parenthood and my very special son have taught me a thing or two. I think parents have a chance, after an intense training period and after lots and lots of failure, of coming close to genius when there's a situation that involves picking and choosing moments: when to praise, when to discipline, when to just plain stay out of it. I have learned—the hard way, and only occasionally—how to get a grip, and how to stave off feeling sorry for myself.

I move into the dining room as the winter black stretches into daylight, as the chilly Northwest sunrise with its oranges and lavenders and golds sends a glow through every window in our little house. I peer out and see the solstice stars, twinkling from their pastel stations high above. An excited little pajama-clad urchin won't come staggering out for a few hours, and that seems like all the time in the world. I slip the portable compact disc player into the pocket of my fuzzy bathrobe and position the headphones on my ears: a radiant-voiced choir begins its festival of song. One by one, I light the candles, a dozen of them, my favorite tall ones, fat ones, votives, all in white. And while carols ring in my head, sung only for me, there at last is my Christmas house. The fat jolly tree, the candles burning steadily, and sparse walls—without a single satin ribbon or wreath or sprig of holly or greeting card display or extra added attraction—where the shadows can choreograph their dance. One shining moment for me alone, a treasure brought in with the dawn, as the sugarplum boy dreams his dreams a few feet away.

The sun is almost up in all its December glory. I know that in a little while, I'll blow the candles out and leave not a trace of my pleasure. William will be up, greeting the morning with ebullient shouts and leaps as he has on every Christmas morning since he was two. The stage is set for him, and perhaps that is how it should be; he's the little one. I stand in the frosty window and feel Christmas all around me. And I think: Will is my cause for celebration. Will is my reason for joy. He just can't join me right now.

Hero

It was as if I knew the moment would happen before it came. I had a premonition.

As I was taking Will to the car at the end of the school day, his first-grade teacher ran up to me. "Kelly! Kelly, I need to tell you something." She put her hand on my shoulder. "The principal will be calling you today. There's been a problem. We found out about a situation with some kids harassing Will. I wanted to talk to you about it right away!"

I had been living in some kind of crystal bubble and now came the sound of shattering glass. I thought, This is it. We're in public school. This is the start of it all.

The children guilty of the harassment had been brought to the principal's office that very day. Three first-grade boys, just little boys. The principal asked them why they'd done it. "Because we knew he wouldn't be able to tell," one of them said.

What had happened was that every time Will went into a stall in the boys' room, the other boys got into the stall and pushed him around. The teacher wasn't sure where he had been touched. It had happened quite a few times. Will wasn't able to lock the stall door. His fingers didn't work that way. He couldn't defend himself with words or anything else. He didn't have even a semblance of the skills to help him defend himself against the boys—who were really just being boys. But the thought of those boys put my heart in a vice.

The following day I met with the principal, Ms. Clark, in her office. We decided that a teacher or an aide would check on Will whenever he went to the bathroom. Ms. Clark thought that Will's teacher should call her students together in a circle, while Will was in a Special Ed room doing one-on-one, for a meeting about "Privacy." The school had conducted such meetings before. We came up with the idea of getting the on-site occupational therapist to help Will learn to operate the lock on the stall door.

This was the strategy, all laid out in serious tones, a way to cope, and I was grateful—deeply grateful—for the quick action and the high level of concern. Yet a selfish little voice inside me was begging—what about me? How do I protect myself? The answer was already growing, in fact, in the form of a shell around my heart. This first incident—or, the first one I knew about—could have turned out to be much worse. We were at an excellent school. So many of the kids were kind and sweet. To try to watch over Will, I would need to check in more often. I would need to communicate more with his teachers. But in order to shield myself from what might be lurking around the next corner of the brick wall of elementary school, middle school, high school—if we made it that far—I imagined I would have to develop a tougher skin.

And another thought closer to the surface was: who had discovered the culprits? A teacher, I assumed—one of the teachers must have walked in while it was happening. No, said the principal, it had been a child. In fact it was another boy from Will's class who had gone to their teacher to tell the story. But as all the names involved with the incident were being kept anonymous, Ms. Clark wished to keep that boy's name a secret as well.

Yet that boy was my salvation, he was my hope. Was it possible that there were first graders in the world with such a strong sense of what was right? Maybe I just didn't know enough about "normal" kids, but I was surprised to find out that a classmate had come to Will's rescue. After the meeting with Ms. Clark I went to peek into Will's room. Who was it? I wanted to send a big bouquet to his door, with a special letter thanking him and his parents too, for raising a son who, so early in life, understood the importance of helping another kid. And more than that, I wanted to express my thanks to them all for giving me a reason to let go of the dreadful, desolate feelings I'd felt at the idea of fending off such cruelty on a regular basis. When I realized that there was a child like this mystery kid in Will's class, I couldn't help but rejoice that empathy could exist even in the heart of a six-year-old.

Of course, I had a feeling it was Eric. He stood out, with his dark brown doe-eyes and his sensitive manner. Once I saw him try to help Will, try to play with him on the playground. These are the kinds of things that become etched in the heart and memory of a mom like me. He was my first guess, and the right one. I knew his mother from chats in the school hallway, I even had her phone number in my book. When I called, she said, "Yes, it was Eric."

I knew I must sit Will down and talk to him about the incident when what I really wanted was to whisk him off to Fiji for the rest of the school year, where we would run on the beach and crack open coconuts together and decide, maybe, never to return home. "Did the boys hurt you?" "No." Did the boys bother you?" "Yes." "Well, if they do it again, you can tell the teacher. And we will teach you how to close the door on the toilet stall so you can keep them out." I tried to give suggestions, without playing the whole thing up too much, though I wasn't sure I was getting through. He seemed to have survived what had happened without any psychological scars. It had bugged him a little, that was all. But the same boys harassed him again a few weeks later. A teacher who was on the lookout for trouble walked in on the scene. Their parents had been contacted the first time, and now they were contacted again, and I came in for another meeting with Ms. Clark. But I didn't cry in her office as I had the first time. I was able to garner a little more strength as I spoke to her about reinforcing our strategy.

I found Eric in front of the door to class a week or so after the second upset. I stopped him and put my hand on his little shoulder. "Thank you, Eric, thank you so much—I know you came to Will's rescue," I told him. "Oh, yeah!" He looked up at me with huge eyes. "Yeah," he said again.

From his mom, I got hold of Eric's smiling class picture from that year and tacked it to the bulletin board on our refrigerator. And there it remains.

One Dream

I pass through my kitchen and notice a mishmash of photos taped to the refrigerator door. They've been stuck up in the same place forever it seems, and now the corners have yellowed and the tape is coming off. These tattered prints were cut from magazines years ago; they show pictures of beautiful waterfront homes sitting on hillsides, gorgeous rustic dream houses set among misty pines, overlooking lakes, resting over ponds. The houses peek out at me from the crazy fridge-collage of magnetic alphabet letters and PTA reminders and baby photos haphazardly displayed on the white door—as in so many family kitchens, the refrigerator acts as our home's official kiosk. There was once a dream there, in those little clippings. A fantasy that I could taste. The smell of new pine flooring. The scent of smoke from a river rock fireplace. The feel of a lakefront breeze sweeping over a deck where I could stand out in my bathrobe and slippers and breathe in the fragrant morning air. Where I could be silent, listening for the flap and call of Canada geese. I dreamed of homes, of living rooms full of furniture, of gardens of herbs and English roses.

But now I gaze at the pictures and they seem like an obsession from a very faraway time. I have other things on my mind today. I have a different dream. I've forgotten perfect houses, furniture, linen, china, landscaped gardens, the Martha Stewart lifestyle. That was my magazine world. In it my mind was free to travel to quaint European villages and dip my toes in the turquoise waters of the Caribbean. I could extend the vision and imagine myself a supermodel in Armani, relaxing in a tapestry chair. Staring at my refrigerator, I wonder when I ever had time to go to that place. Or the motivation, even.

Oh, I can still travel off to fantasyland every now and again. And I wouldn't have to be dragged hollering and kicking into the real-life version of that fabulous world. But the material dream is no longer the dream I hold high. It isn't the thing that presses me forward, the goal that burns in my heart. Something took over. Something pushed magazine dreams right out of my head.

It's the dream that my son will be happy, and will find a way to move comfortably through this world.

When you have one big overpowering dream, a mother's dream, nothing gets in the way of it. It has top priority at all times. It's as urgent as a baby's cry.

A friend of mine who has amassed many dollars (and who has remained one of the kindest, best people in my life), once told me how he could pick up on people's feelings so easily, how he could tell when they were envious of his money. But could he have guessed my feelings? While we were on a tour of his House Beautiful, a fairyland compound set among acres and acres of forest, his four-year-old boy rushed up to us and asked his dad in a chirp for a quarter. Such a passing moment, such a normal kid-like thing. Because I had never heard such a quick, spontaneous, lucid request from my own child of the same age, my entire body ached with envy. It isn't a bank account, it's a word I'm jealous of: *ease*.

When Will and I enter into a relationship with a new teacher or a therapist or a camp counselor or even a babysitter, that poor unsuspecting individual is viewed as a potential dream-maker. What doors are they capable of unlocking? Do they hold the key to our happiness? Do they have what it takes to open door upon door? My dreams are patient ones, and as it turns out, we have found that magic and that friendship in many people along the way. And they may never know how many seeds they helped plant in our little dream-garden.

Parents of kids like mine, from what I have witnessed in my years of being part of the community, possess a constant high level of concern for their children's ultimate success, or, in some cases, even survival. If our children are in school for the day, we literally can't let go of the idea of what might be happening in the classroom, of what they may or may not be taking in, of how they are responding from hour to hour. If they are in therapy, we spend the time praying that when they emerge from the session they will have come up even a tiny notch in their progress. When we're with them we keep a careful watch, we intervene, we try to stay keenly aware of how much it takes to meet their needs, like the parents of newborns. Or we may guiltily try to give ourselves a break by letting them play a repetitive game off in a corner somewhere, but really we are incapable of giving ourselves a break, for there is always more to try to figure out, so much more to be done. There is always, always more, even when we don't have a clue what it is that we can do.

We reach, we strive, and it's all for one dream.

I go on the Internet and search for parent groups. I follow up on every phone number that people in their kindness pass on to me. I sit on the floor in front of the Special Needs shelf in the mega-bookstore and read every book. Will talks about eventually living in an apartment, so I'm continually saying to him: "When you get your apartment…" "When you get your apartment, you'll need to know how to open a jar. Come on, let's practice." "When you get your apartment, you'll have to know how to put your shirt on right-side-out. Here, let's learn!"

Little steps toward the big dream.

These days, out in the country at my mother-in-law's house, I wander down a needle-strewn path overlooking a silvery inlet, and I stand in the breeze and breathe the pine air, watching and listening for the waterfowl. Back at my own house I'm perfectly happy when I can pull together an ersatz magazine outfit from the old clothes in my closet. My husband and I have talks about the long exotic vacation we'll take alone…one day. And we're content with our modest home because it is surrounded by a dozen neighbors who care about our son, who know us as a family and support us right down the line. I have everything I need. It's what William needs that interests me, that drives me, now.

The fluffy towels and embroidered quilts and the set of copper pots—I think they are for someone else.

I have a dream so much more complex. I've moved everything else away. I've set everything else aside. My mind needs to be clear, so I can concentrate.

Evolution Blues

Mississippi Doggone Whatever-His-Name-Is shouts in a growl from the speakers over our heads. My husband and I hold each other in a teen-like embrace, rocking awkwardly back and forth to the music, moving our heavy feet just a half-inch or so—left, right, left, right. Guitar riffs blare in short bursts, drums pound, and the mirror-ball above us sends rainbow dots circling around the dance hall in the dark. Tiny colored stars race over the yellow plank floor and all around the walls postered with black-and-white pictures of Fred Astaire. "Just to say hello my little darling—do you remember me? Now it's been a great long time, I just wanna let you see," sings Howlin' Memphis or whoever the gruff, soulful voice belongs to. The music, all blues, is fabulous, the sound system is state of the art. The other dancing couples surrounding us seem perfectly comfortable, and this is only the first dance lesson of the eight-week series.

Charles and I, however, have a long way to go.

"Just an eee-zy rock, back and forth, back and forth," calls out Sean, the teacher, also known as "Gator." He wears one of those head-phone-microphone devices like Janet Jackson. "This is the basic step. These are baby steps, everybody go ahead and take it slow. We're just going to do this for awhile." Easy for him to say—he's a tall, strapping blonde with, it's apparent from the first beat, incredible grace and confidence. Gator has a partner, MaryLee. They are a reputable team. I did a lot of research before we ended up here, shyly swaying under the lights like a boy and girl who've never met before.

Accidentally, I step on Charlie's toe. He hadn't wanted to come this class. I was really living in a dream to think he would ever want to get up in front of people and practice dance moves, no matter how hip the music. Who could blame him? I set it all up as a surprise, believing it would be just the thing to get romance back into our romance-deprived lives. But I had apprehensions myself. In our entire marriage we had danced publicly but once or twice, and those times stood out as being somewhat humiliating—it turned out we were two professional music makers who managed to completely lose our gift of rhythm out on the dance floor.

It had been a quiet ride to the dance studio. "You're sure you want to do this class," he sighed under his breath as we got into the car. I usually have to move mountains to get a babysitter when we need one. Now I'd moved an entire range in order to procure one for eight Tuesdays in a row. "Yes," I said. The rest of the ride was spent in silence.

At the door, Charles began to feel ill. We were moving up in the registration line and had almost reached a beautiful woman, another dance official, whose name tag read "Selah" and who was taking checks at the sign-in table. "My stomach is bothering me," he said to me. I nudged him through the line. "Honey, it's going to be okay," I said.

When I first broke the news that I wanted to enroll us in this cool-sounding dance class with the quirky title "Evolution Blues," I didn't have to go far to remind him that dancing to blues songs was the cornerstone of our courtship. We had been living together in an old apartment building on Roy Street in a trendy neighborhood in Seattle and every Sunday night the local jazz station would play an evening of blues. We stood in the living room window by lamplight and danced. Of course, given our innate problems, you probably couldn't call it dancing. But whatever it was—bumping, shuffling, tripping—it produced the sexiest, most powerful feeling of romance I'd ever known. Neither one of us could possibly forget that it was perhaps the first way we deeply connected with one another.

That was why the light bulb went off when I heard about this class through a friend. Now here we are, on a fairly crowded floor, in front of everyone, feeling exactly like Laurel and Hardy. "Hello, speak to me," cries the blues singer in a storm of passion. "I been wonderin' where can my little darling be? It's been such a great long time, darlin', do you remember me?" The track pulses loudly. MaryLee strides past us—she's got a matching little headpiece like Gator's. "Just relax, you guys," she whispers. She touches my back. Are we that obvious?

Relaxing does not come easily to two people who basically live their lives at home trying to meet the needs of one very demanding little boy. Our evenings consist of lots of repetition, lots of routine. The same conversations, over and over again, dozens of times a night. Will: "The Chelan ferry looks the same as the Kitsap!" Dad: "Yes." Will: "The Tacoma ferry looks the same as the Wenatchee!" Mom: "Yes." The same kid videos we have watched for six years play in the background of our home, for perhaps their two-hundred-and-fiftieth viewing—we have a heck of a time getting him hooked on a new one. Will can go off on his own a little, but not a lot: mostly one of us is entertaining him while the other heads to a different room for a private moment. All of this along with balancing schedules, worrying about school, wondering about the future. This class is one of the first times in ages we've had a chance to be alone together, focusing on something other than our charge. As a couple, as a Fred and Ginger, it would be accurate to say we're a little rusty.

I look around at the other dancers. There are couples in their twenties, and others who are silver-haired. Everyone looks happy. How many are parents, I wonder, with babysitters at home? How many are taking this class as a form of stress management? Charles and I are like all moms and dads, I think: dying for a break in the established program.

"Do you remember me?" Blind Daddy Whoever yells in powerful tones as the song ends. I'm a singer myself and I can't believe I don't recognize the voice of this great artist. But the music has definitely moved both my partner and me to a new place. I feel Charlie's body loosen as we continue to hold each other, getting ready to hear Gator's next directive. "On this next song push your hips together with your partner's in a little grinding motion. And—we're going to try a dip!" comes the teacher's amplified call. My eyes meet my husband's in a look of panic. But then, we break into laughter.

There are times when our son comes home from school and he shows us his math test with a big red "100%" splashed across the top and we glance at each other in a certain way, a glance that is a mixture of surprise, relief, over-the-moon pride, and glowing satisfaction, and only Charles can know what's in my heart, and only I can know his joy.

Or we look at each other as we stifle our individual giggles, as when we saw Will sitting at the dining room table the other night with a white mound covering the sheet of paper in front of him. "What are you doing?" one of us asked. He held up a little glass saltshaker. "I'm salting my homework," he replied, smiling with the familiar raised eyebrow.

But there is another kind of look we've been missing. The one where Charlie's eyes narrow and stare straight into mine. And it is as if we are suddenly on a misty film set with a computerized moon and special effect stars. And music plays. Lately there hasn't been a time or a place, it seems, for that look to come back to us. We once played lovers in the movie, before we became Mom and Dad, and it's the lovers' look that was somehow deleted from the script. Tonight we had to talk ourselves into climbing the wooden steps that lead to this hidden dancehall in a poorly lit back alley above a restaurant. But now we're caught up in the blues again, like in the old days. We may have finally found the time, and the place.

The lithesome Gator, who also spins the discs, hops up to the DJ booth in the corner of the studio. "We just heard Lightnin' Hopkins," he announces, "with 'Do You Remember Me Blues.' You're looking good, everyone. Here's Muddy Waters." He must not have been watching the sorry duo in the back. But when the next driving intro rings out over the room, I notice that my suddenly-very-attractive partner and I have a bit more style going. We've got the basic move. I give a nod to the couple next to us. Left, right, left, right, bump, grind, dip. Charles has a smile on his face. I feel like we're back on Roy Street. Maybe this was a good idea, after all.

Over Washington

Beneath us, fields of green roll toward the sparkling sea. We fly rapidly, steadily. Hundreds of feet below, a miniature lighthouse moves into our bird's-eye view, standing brightly at the end of a spit, amid a cluster of tiny, pristine white buildings. Sailboats are lined up on the water and their pin-sized masts bob in the sun. We sweep and dip and fly forward, and now we're over a city. This is Will's favorite part of the video, as we almost touch the spindle-top of the Space Needle, and are allowed a few seconds to look for landmarks. But in a moment we've sailed past; once again we're looking down on dots of cattle grazing on a patchwork plain.

Is this the perfect entertainment for my kid or what? When I first discovered it one evening on PBS, I was overjoyed. Will has always seen things from above. If you ask him to draw a house—well, forget the windows, the pointed roof and the door, the classic kiddie's sun and rainbow at the top of the picture. Will draws the overhead floor plan of a house, and always has. He is now famous in our family for sketching overhead maps on his dry-erase board—schools, neighborhoods, the insides of ferryboats, playgrounds, malls. They are always perfectly and accurately rendered, like something you'd see on an architect's drawing table. And it makes so much sense. To confront things head-on—well, this is the most unimaginably difficult thing my child has to face in the world. How much easier it is to avoid the confrontation, the intrusion, by lifting oneself up, and over and out, and trying to get at the situation from a completely different angle.

So we fly. I like to turn down the New Age-y piano music and watch in silence, and so does Will, I think. There are no threats to us here, as we move Over Washington, because there is no time—a thing is there and then it's gone. Of course, whereas my son still finds the scenery interesting after repeated showings, I may space out a little here and there. I go on my own journey, a journey of my past.

★ ★ ★

I settled in the Northwest after one day checking out a stack of books from the library in my hometown of L.A. There, in glossy pictures provided by Sunset magazine photographers, I saw the same green hills and blue lakes that roll before me in the video. I knew the trees already, from summers with my parents in Oregon. There was nothing like the fragrance of old-growth forest, nothing like the light of god-rays filtering through the hanging moss. Tall pines and snowcapped mountains beckoned. And even though I had a huge dream of making it as a singer in my Hollywood hometown, I couldn't resist the call. I was barely twenty years old, but I knew I had to travel north and put down new roots.

My first stop in Washington was on an island. In many an island cabin, on the wall by the front door, or for sale in the local souvenir shops, there is a framed print of a poem that reads: "If once you have slept on an island, you'll never be quite the same." And it's so true. I didn't last long on my green isle—I was a city girl and Seattle won out in the end—but when the Over Washington videocam lifts me over and through the San Juans, emerald forms floating on a silver sea, I become a sentimental time-traveler.

I did make a career of music in Seattle, as a big fish in a small pond, and it suited me. Music ended up taking me around the world, in fact, so I suppose I finally got to swim in a bigger pool. For years I never gave one thought to having a child. I didn't want any kids, really. I went through my twenties and almost all of my thirties with a plan, basically, to *not* have a baby. I vividly remember once standing at the sink doing the dishes and looking around at my lovely peaceful Seattle house, when the thought that must at some point cross everyone's mind came into my head. Something I'd seen in the newspaper about a disabled child had sparked it. What would happen, I wondered for a split second, if I had a baby and there was something wrong with it? The horror every woman chooses to put right out of her mind. No, I had a nice home and my chosen field of music to fill me up. I didn't have to think about such things. Of course, I hadn't met my husband yet—that part of my tale was yet to unfold.

★   ★   ★

Sailing down the majestic coastline. We glide in silence. At the edge of the ocean we zoom in close on mystical rock formations. The Northwest held so many stories for me. It was my destiny to come here. Now I see it.

★   ★   ★

Will was a golden, curly-haired baby when I used to rock him to the rhythm of a Shawn Colvin song: "I love you baby/I can see you and I/as we fly away together/up to Orion in the sky." Of the hours of music we would listen to, this was our favorite track, and we'd stand in the living room with the stereo turned up. I must have known something about Will's urge to fly, even then. I held him tightly as we waltzed together, and felt an incredible bonding as we listened to words about soaring together to the stars. "Maybe somewhere in the southern hemisphere/ there can be room for all this love/where they've saved a place for innocence/and what is still mysterious…." I think it was supposed to be a song about the environment, yet it spoke to the mother in me so profoundly, as baby and I rocked back and forth with our eyes closed and his cheeks like the softest duck-down next to mine.

★ ★ ★

Now the great River Columbia is glimmering, rolling, and we can almost touch it. Within minutes we've popped up to higher heights, and we're looking down upon craggy, frosted mountain peaks, the ethereal Cascade Range. We move so fast. Will coasts along, but he's not much for nature. He's waiting for another city, Spokane maybe, or better yet another cruise over Seattle, where he can catch one more glimpse of toy-like white ferries on a sapphire Puget Sound.

"So I'll see you darlin'/Now fly, baby fly/Down across the Fiji Islands/To where the Seven Sisters cry/Gather all your dreams and take them somewhere so far out of reach...."

When he was a brand-new bud of possibility, light as a little package, how we would rock, and dance.

It feels fantastic to be way up here, gliding over the lush beauty of the state, skimming its surface, soaring effortlessly above the world. We could stay here forever, but we won't. The videotape will buzz to an end in the VCR machine. William and I will land together on the mossy ground. We'll have to handle the adjustment, deal with the terrain. He seems to have been born with a natural ability to tell north from south, east from west. He knows so much; he'll take me where I need to go. We'll climb the mountains, and follow the winding trail through the forest, under the ancient, sheltering cedars.

Willpower

Special Needs Showbiz

Will knows what he wants to be when he grows up. He wants to be a ferryboat worker for the Washington State Ferry System. In fact, Will, now age fifteen, has always looked to the future with confidence and gusto. Once when he was seven years old and we were out driving, he saw a brick apartment building he loved because it overlooked the city. He decided he would like to live there someday, so I took down the address. A year or two later, while still in grade school, he started a short list of high schools he might like to attend. We would visit the buildings on weekends to see what they looked like. At the top of Will's list was a neighborhood institution, Roosevelt High School, a grand 1922 terra- cotta-trimmed landmark that stood high on a hill, reigning over the housetops like a queen. The moment Will saw it he wanted it in his life. He seemed so sure of these things.

I have something in common with this young thinker. At the age of eight I made up my mind to be a professional singer, and unlike my son who can remember the date and time of anything, I'm not that brilliantly blessed. But I remember the cloth napkins, the gleaming silver bowls of sugar cubes, the potted palms and the tapestry chairs of the Ambassador Hotel in L.A. on the morning my mother took me to meet Shirley Temple. The former ringleted doll of film legend (who'd grown up to be a beautiful lady who hosted fairy tales on TV) was making an appearance at a charity breakfast in one of the hotel banquet rooms. My mother knew that I lived for her; I sang her movie songs around the house all the time. I'd put on one of Mom's short little nightgowns, don my treasured tap shoes, and recreate "On the Good Ship Lollipop" and other routines for my parents on our linoleum kitchen floor. Now the real Shirley shimmered before me, giving her speech from the podium, and when she was finished I gobbled down the last of my French toast, took my mother's hand and trounced over to wait in the long autograph line. When my turn came I stood there marveling at her black hair, her red lips, the collar of her grey silk suit, and as she scribbled in my pink plastic book with the poodle on the cover, something seized me. "I sing all your songs!" I blurted out shamelessly. She handed back the book and looked straight at me. "Oh, you're a singer!" she smiled, the famous dimples thrilling my heart. And that was that. She turned to sign a napkin for another tiny seeker, but Shirley Temple had spoken, and right away I understood my life's calling.

From then on, like my son, I focused narrowly on one thing. It was my dream to be a performer, and the dream came true. By my teens I was warbling my heart out for real audiences in real venues; in my twenties I made records and traveled the world. And in the midst of the music I soon got attached to the package—the glamor and the lights, the adventure and the applause—that was all a part of show business. I was born for it. No matter the hard knocks, I went forward with ambition and fortitude, taking the thrills with the rejection, and learning the tools of a long-established trade.

When, many years into this work, Will came along (I became pregnant at forty), it took but an instant to realize that a new talent was going to nudge me out of the spotlight—the kid was a natural. And when the shining star of my life was diagnosed with autism, I felt Ms. Entertainment taking what perhaps might be her final bow. The song of showbiz was fading like a meaningless lyric. I had a whole new set of skills to learn.

Yet I discovered something. The old tricks, the ones I'd acquired on the stage and along the road, still came in handy, came to the rescue in fact, in my new job. So what if the challenges that loomed before me as a mother were more intimidating than any audience I had ever faced? I was a pro, and the show would go on.

For instance, in the park, in a store, on the playground, anywhere in public, Will might be joyfully squawking out his baby-like syllables at top volume or, on the other hand, exploding in a tantrum at the same high decibel. Dozens of people would look over at us and stare. But it was something I'd grown used to a long time ago. A throng of folks, watching me, curious and critical? That was normal.

In the parent support groups I was the warm-up act, the comedienne. As the curtain went up on a chorus line of grieving moms and dads, I'd jump in and begin the meeting by yakking my heart out in a rush of emotion, or tell a funny icebreaker story about something Will had done that day. The evening would get off to a great start. Other mothers, more timid than me perhaps, would begin to open up.

The stories I told at the meetings grew into stories for the preschool newsletter; from there they were published in a book, and with the book came book signings and personal appearances, which I handled, naturally, with effervescence and aplomb. It was not lost on me that this new life of storytelling, though begun from a place of heartache and deep love for my child, was also benefiting beautifully from a type of strategy I once used all the time when I was selling myself, armed with demo tapes and 8 ×10 glossies.

In the world of parenting children with special needs, you tap into all of yourself, even parts you never knew existed. I wasn't sacrificing the life that was in my blood. I was practicing it like never before.

★ ★ ★

At a lecture I gave to promote my book, I first got the scoop on Roosevelt High School. A classroom assistant in Roosevelt's autism program came up to me at the end of my talk and introduced herself. As soon as she mentioned where she was from and started talking about her job, I froze at attention. "It's the greatest program you can imagine," she told me. "It's run by a woman who is an expert in the field—it would be so perfect for your son!" Will was only a fifth-grader at the time, but the fifth-grader himself had taught me that it wasn't too soon to fantasize.

I had a million questions for this girl, but before I could begin asking them the chirp in her tone turned cautious. "Unfortunately the class is full, and we've got an endless waiting list—I know it's several years long at the moment." She saw my face fall, and she tried to chirp again. "But you never know!"

Oh, but I did know. I knew then and there that I had four years to put together an act.

In the meantime, Will's father and I needed to find a middle school with an autism program, and we were lucky enough to discover a wonderful one in the public school district, where Will had spent his successful elementary school life. It was called Salmon Bay School, and securing a seat there took a bit of work—autism and Asperger's students were starting to come up through the system in shockingly big numbers, and the few classes that had been designed to serve them filled up fast. Parents of kids like mine had to search hard for good placements, start early, interview teachers and get to know principals. But eventually Will was enrolled at Salmon Bay. The teachers were brilliant, and they determined that, since Will really didn't operate at grade level, he would need basic reading and math skills, plus as many social opportunities as the staff could devise. He was mainstreamed into a few regular classes (and enjoyed all the fabulous fun activities the school was known for—art, sports, community service) and given one-on-one tutoring in his autism classroom. He worked as a teacher's assistant in the school library. He thrived. Salmon Bay was heaven, and we were spoiled.

One day, two years before graduation from his perfect middle school, Will and I took a drive over to Roosevelt High. The entire complex was in the midst of a spectacular remodel, and we knew that it would have its grand opening in the fall of Will's freshman year. It was going to be a showplace. As we drove slowly past the main building, where old brown brick was being sandblasted to its original amber beauty, I felt a longing in my heart. I'd already checked in with several parents whose kids were in the amazing autism program. They said they were the happiest parents in the world—and there were no seats available. "I'm going there," said Will.

What did I used to do as an aspiring vocalist pounding the pavement? How did I finally get to the place where I felt on top of the world, singing with some of the greatest names in the music industry?

With a list of potential backers taped to my refrigerator—teachers, principals, therapists and every school official with whom I had made acquaintance during the course of Will's education—I started networking, two years in advance. I made phone calls and sent emails: I let it be known what I was after. By the time we were one year away from middle school graduation, a couple of teachers were already on the case without my even knowing it. One was Colleen, an instructional assistant at Salmon Bay, who, in a little miracle, happened to be friends with the head of the Roosevelt program, Dr. Candi Styer, whose greatness had been described to me years before by the assistant at my lecture. Colleen loved Will and had already been talking him up to her friend. My other agent was a teacher at Roosevelt, a wonderful man who knew Will through the community and me through my book. He called out of the blue one day to tell me he thought there might be a way—a long shot, a chance—to get Will into his school. He couldn't say much more, but he gave me names and numbers and encouraged me to set up meetings as soon as possible. He would be on my side.

Of course school district policy was based, as it should be, on the idea of fairness to one and all. Our family along with other families would fill out an application naming our school choices, and a district panel would make the final decision for each student based on a number of different factors. There were no special strings one could pull, and yet sometimes there were: in certain cases parents hired lawyers to change the district's mind and often they were successful. I charged ahead and organized my meetings. The first would be with the autism classroom goddess herself, Candi Styer. The other was with the special education director at Roosevelt High School. Last but far from least was a meeting with the key man, the head honcho of special education at the school district.

Candi, who immediately struck me as the mentor for my son that I'd been looking for all his life, showed me around her classroom (the entire school had been moved to an interim site during the big remodel) and I saw what I wanted to see. The situation would fit Will like a glove. The group of about eight students were busy learning money math, working on their computers, getting ready to go grocery shopping with student tutors who'd been recruited from around the school, and a few older ones were even heading off to their part-time jobs in the community. Will, were he to achieve his dream of attending Roosevelt, would be mainstreamed into a few regular classes as well and be able to feel like he was a real part of things. My heart leapt at the thought of it. I shook Candi's hand, maybe too hard, and went on to my next meeting with the high school's special ed administrator, who gave me his full attention as I extolled the virtues of my son. When I left the building I felt, for some strange reason, empowered, and I practically flew to my car. Even though nothing had changed numbers-wise—there still wasn't a seat available for Will and it was unrealistic to think there would be—I was far from ready to give up. These were such good people and teachers. They were listening to me.

Then, a few days later on my way to meet with the top school official, I started getting a bad case of stage fright. As I pulled into the parking lot of the district offices I knew I was just another parent pleading her case. Who did I think I was? Someone with a child more deserving than other shining boys and girls I knew in the autism world? All I knew was that my son had drawn maps of Roosevelt High since he was eight. That once a week he made me drive him over to the new construction site and let him get out of the car so he could gaze over the land and monitor how it was all coming along; and that each time we did this he stood on the sidewalk of the busy street and launched into a little jig that he and I fondly called "The Roosevelt Dance." The whole idea of attending this school when it was finally finished, huge and brand-new and exciting, brought Will to some elevated, nirvana-like state. Now my own state was one of nerves, but thinking about Will's dance gave me courage, and I got out of my car.

I stepped bravely into The Man's office, wearing the sparkling face of public relations and carrying an autographed copy of my book of stories about Will. As the honcho scribbled notes on a yellow legal pad, looking down at the paper the whole time, I performed my honey- drenched, yet truthful, monologue: so far, my son had experienced a close-to-idyllic life in the school system; public school had so much more to offer Will than even the private schools his father and I had, over the years, gone to see. We wanted to continue our wonderful school experience at Roosevelt, which was a perfectly appropriate setting for the next phase of Will's education. Didn't The Man agree that made sense? I'd visited every other possible high school program in the city and Roosevelt was the best fit. "In fact, it's the only fit," I stated with fake confidence because by then I really wanted to weep over his desk. Still, I held myself together the way a solid performer must as the official continued scribbling on his pad and nodding his head. Finally he looked up at me. "The Roosevelt classroom has no opening at this time," he said. Yes, I knew that, I told him quietly. He nicely suggested I go back and look at some other schools. I left. And as I wandered through the office corridors and out into the city sunlight I thought: But what about The Roosevelt Dance?

I stood in the parking lot, dejected. I was a number, and all the numbers were worthy of an equal shot, that was certainly true. But here I was, back to my pavement pounding days. The bigwigs had the power. The competition was fierce. My client's whole career was in the hands of an invisible mogul.

I called Dr. Styer one more time. "I want you to know something," she said to me. "There is a possibility that I could take Will as an 'overload' student, which means there would be no compensation for having this extra student in my classroom. That's the only way. And it might not be able to happen, but if it did—I would make that decision. I could add him to the class if I felt the situation was right."

Her words filled my heart, and I remembered from some other part of my life what it meant to go for broke. I took a trip to the office supply store and bought an electric blue folder; I came home and sifted through photos of Will and found a few killer shots that captured his winning aura, his magical smile. I typed out a letter to Dr. Styer. I told her that to accept Will into her program would not only benefit her as a teacher, it would enrich the lives of the kids in her class and many of the students at the high school as well. I quoted praise for the boy from some of the heavyweight backers whose names were on my fridge; I included a map Will had drawn of his dream school. I tore over to Roosevelt and left my promotional package, with Will's name in big letters on the front, on Candi's desk. Overload. I had not heard the term before, but I clung to it.

Soon after, through a team effort by the Salmon Bay teachers and me, diplomatic visits were arranged. Candi came to Will's class at middle school to observe him at work; Will visited her room at Roosevelt. Will was keenly aware of the stakes and rose to the occasion—you couldn't have asked for more successful summits if you were Jimmy Carter. But at last the hard sell was over, and there was nothing to do but wait.

It would be months before the school placements were announced, via official letters dropped in the mailboxes of anxious families (by mail carriers who could not know they held the future in their hands). I had dutifully filled out our school choice form and sent it in, as one of a multitude of deserving hopefuls. Will's teachers at Salmon Bay, who had done much to support me in my campaign, crossed their fingers. And I did my best to teach Will the merits of patience while trying to teach myself the same thing. One day, even before the letter arrived, I received an email from an anonymous source. I didn't know who the sender was, but, having worked as long and hard on this case as I had, I knew I had connections in high places. "Ms. Harland," read the message, "In a day or two you should be receiving your letter of high school placement for your son. I think you will be pleased."

A show-stopping moment.

The next day our letter arrived. I tore it open. Will, fearful of devastating news, covered his ears when I started to tell him. I had to shout to get him to hear: "It's Roosevelt, Will! You are going to be a student at Roosevelt High School!"

He whooped and hollered for half an hour. He jumped up and down like a kangaroo.

That year as the autumn leaves were turning color in a silvery mist, I dropped Will off in front of his magnificent new high school for the first day of classes. He slammed the car door with a "Bye, Mom," sprinted up the sweeping stairs to the entrance, pulled open a mahogany door and slipped inside. There went my unstoppable son, off to Candi's classroom and everything it had to offer him. I looked across the rolling green lawn where a stone tablet announced the school's motto in engraved gothic letters: "What I am to be, I am now becoming." I know what made me into a happy little songbird. It wasn't pow-wowing with the powers-that-be. I was like my son. I believed in dreams, and I had a dream that called me, and nothing could take it away.

A Mountaintop in Nepal

I've tried to explain to Will about the hate, violence, and horrors of the world. He just doesn't get it.

The boy who lives in my house would be the perfect specimen for a research study of teens who have never been touched by the media culture. It might be hard to round up such a study group. Perhaps the research would begin and end with my kid.

Here is an intelligent young man who, due to his problem in processing information, can only look at a few slow-moving videos or DVDs, all of which are of the most benign content. He loves looking at videos of himself as a baby or as a kindergartner, or watching home movies of his train trips and ferry excursions (he currently shoots them himself, complete with long-winded narration). One of the few actual films he's seen is a video we found in a bookstore one day, entitled "The Sound of Ferries." For thirty-five minutes we can watch the big Seattle boats going peacefully back and forth, back and forth, back and forth across the water, and that's all there is to it. (I've often wondered if this film has any other fans besides us.)

In other words, we have missed mice hitting cats over the heads with frying pans. We have missed earthlings battling aliens from outer space. We have lived without wars, witches, monsters. We never got the news that Bambi's mother died or had to search for Nemo. Will missed the training period, when a seed gets planted in the heads of wee ones, warning them there's danger ahead, that it's not all nursery rhymes and Dr. Seuss.

As for video games, Will does play them—but car races only. He'll maneuver his high-speed hot rod along the endless highway, through European villages, the jungle, the desert; he'll explore our colorful world at a hundred miles an hour. He loves the speed and he'll play for hours, but no one blows anyone up. There are crashes here and there and a couple of bursts of flame, but there are no swords, no guns, no villains, no killing. At this point in his life, Will could never step out from behind the driver's wheel and follow the pack into the popular worlds of boys—whether it be "Lord of the Rings," "Star Wars," or kingdoms much more malign—because they are so beyond him. The sound bites on the news, the photos on the front page of the Net when he opens his computer—he doesn't see the scary stories, the disturbing images. He goes straight to the happy website for Washington State Ferries to see if the Hyak is still in dry dock.

Besides, since he hasn't had more than a few friends his own age, I can't even recall any "bang-bang-you're-dead" games in the sandbox as he was growing up. Hitting, name-calling, having toys wrenched from his hands; there just weren't too many little actors around to play those roles, and if there were there was usually a teacher around to ring down the curtain. And Will barely noticed his pint-sized peers anyway—I wouldn't be able to depend on them to provide my son with clues to humanity's bad side.

He knows there was one terrible day. Every now and then he talks about September 11th because somehow not even little Will missed that one. He realizes that someone did something bad, and that hurting and killing people is wrong. (He doesn't have too many visuals that apply this concept beyond a plane hitting a building, yet I suppose that would be the picture to sum it up for all of us.) But he wouldn't really know how to hate the perpetrators. He doesn't know about religion and he doesn't have a clue that there ever was or ever could be a problem with the color of people's skin. Nor would he think to make fun of an obese person or the homeless man begging on the street in his ragged outfit, or a pierced punk rocker with a rainbow mohawk, or anyone of any size or class or style. He accepts his fellow humans without one ounce of bias or judgment. A few years ago I noticed that along with this acceptance he is actually growing up (in a trait that may go against the autism rulebook) to be keenly interested in them. He won't like it if someone comes along and surprises him out of nowhere, but if given some advance notice and a period of introduction—a chance to see where they work, where their house is, to find out which school they attended and whether they've ever ridden a ferryboat—he opens his heart to people. The extreme pleasure he takes in chatting, in his limited but enthusiastic way, with the neighbor across the street or the checker in our local market never fails to amaze his mother, the bystander.

And so of course, every year, every month, I try to catch him up to the world's evils. "You know, there was a kidnapping the other day," I tell him. "You never know when someone is going to pop out of the bushes and take you away from your parents." He thinks it's hilarious, the idea that someone would pop out of the bushes, like a puppet, and the word "kidnap" strikes him as kind of funny, too. He giggles his head off, and I break into a bit of a sweat. Once again I sit him down with the speech I've been giving him his whole life about what to do if a stranger approaches. I do believe he now understands me when my I've finished my serious-toned lecture; he starts to listen and in the end repeats to me what he's supposed to do if someone he doesn't know comes up to him, or lurks anywhere near. But when we're done discussing it and he's back into his life, he doesn't carry around the low-grade dread people often live with every day of their lives, and it's hard for me not to see that as a quality. Sometimes I even find myself trying to let it rub off on me a little. But then I go back to being soldier-mom.

"Guess what?" I tell him, after finding out that a gunman took out a few shoppers at a mall Will loves to frequent with me, where we run around riding escalators. "A guy came into the mall with a gun! He actually killed some people, Will. We could have been there!"

He's only interested in the exact spot where it all happened. The horrific murder took place at the intersection of two of his favorite department stores—I learned this from the TV news—so he gets very excited and hops around with extreme delight when I tell him it happened between Sears and Penney's.

At last, just the other day, I decided it was time to lay it all out on the table at once: every bad and terrible thing that could happen to a person in the blink of an eye. I'd just group them all together and get it over with. Will was in his bedroom building a high school out of Legos.

"Will, one thing you are going to have to learn is all the bad ways that people can die. You don't even know about all the terrible things that can happen in this world."

He attached another Lego. Click.

"Remember when our neighbor had cancer and you were so upset? Well, she could have died. Cancer is only one of many diseases that kill people. Plus, there are car accidents. We don't know anyone who has been in one, lucky for us! And guns. There are people out there with guns who want money so they kill other people."

"Yeah," he says. "Outside every school there is a sign: No guns or weapons." Meanwhile he had completed his beautiful model of the high school. "Look!" he pointed proudly.

It would have taken two hours to cover my topic. I hadn't even gotten to war. I was already feeling exhausted, and I was starting to depress myself.

There just doesn't seem to be room in our household for thoughts of violence: we are the house of jubilance. Will is all about calendars, the ultimate predictable pursuit, and he celebrates every day as it arrives, fresh, numbered and marked. As the sun comes up (he and his mom are both early risers) he announces the date with anticipation and glee: "It's April 17th!" Every dawn holds the potential of Christmas.

He marvels at rain, hail, snow, sunsets, rainbows, and proclaims their arrival (we have nicknamed him "Moonspotter" and "Rainbowspotter"). He stands at the living room window, his entertainment center, and looks up at the evening sky. "It's a great night for stargazing," he says.

He knows every Beatles' song and sings them all, and if there is anything that spreads more positive energy around the room than the entire Beatles' catalog sung out with a fine musical sensibility and good cheer, I'd like to know what it is.

He loves wordplay and making puns and telling funny stories. He loves to reminisce the great times of his past, especially his preschool days when he says he was happiest of all. Out in the world one can also catch his vibrations and get high. As we stroll through one of Will's favorite department stores he will appear to be floating on air. He'll turn to me and say, "I'm walking on Cloud Nine." Suddenly, in the middle of Target, I am too.

Every few months, of course, we deal with the demons indigenous to Will's disorder—his peculiar moments of panic, sometimes more intense than a lot of things a television screen might show, or situations where his lack of general knowledge is a source of frustration for him and of pain for me. But after these episodes are sorted out and he gathers himself together again, there is a nobility and a courageousness I see in my son that, just as in his jolly times, make him seem wise and wondrous.

When he was two years old and first diagnosed, and life seemed so terribly bleak, friends offered words of encouragement. My friend Libby said: "You know, if Will was born on a mountaintop in Nepal I'll bet he wouldn't even seem different. He would just be kind of magical."

I think back to that comment and I imagine that, because of the way Will is, perhaps this is where our family lives and plays. Somewhere far above society's troubles, high on a mystical lookout where there are no guns or abductions or car bombings. Where we can giggle and make up words and gaze up at the stars, from our mountaintop.

The Broken Leg Diaries

At around 2:30 in the afternoon on November 9th I sat on my bedroom floor, thinking I could challenge a colossal pile of dusty old magazines and forgotten papers to a duel. In the midst of my ridiculously hectic schedule I'd somehow been awarded a minute to breathe, and I was sure I could use that minute to stare the stack of stuff down, and finally get it cleaned up and organized. But in my face-off with the pile, the pile won. I sat motionless on the rug. As I glanced out my window to see gray clouds moving over a gloomy sky, I felt all my energy and focus rolling away with them. I shoved the mess back into its corner, hoisted myself onto the bed, and lay there. "When," I demanded in a sharp whisper, "am I going to be able to just lie down and have someone take care of me?" The question flew out like a fluttering, unbidden little bird, and it surprised me. This was the line moms used all the time as a joke. But exhaled aloud to an empty room, my fed-up sigh held not even a hint of funny.

It was November 9th at 5:30p.m., three hours later in the pitch dark. I scurried down the garden steps to my car, on my way to meet my husband for the rushed romantic dinner we'd planned. I missed a step onto the sidewalk, crashed to the cement, and broke my leg.

There was a confusing, excruciatingly painful five minutes as I screamed for help on the freezing ground ("Hitchcock screams" I would later call them) and then a neighbor rushed to my side, then ten neighbors, then a fire truck and an ambulance. As the ambulance was about to close its doors and roll away from the terror scene ("We've got some bumps coming up," said the medic. "Just squeeze my hand.") I heard Charles' voice close to me. "I'm here, honey! It's okay!" He was leaning in the door of the truck; someone had contacted him, and surely spoiled his appetite for our candlelight meal. He reached in to touch me. My leg felt like it was being stabbed again and again by the sharpest weapon of war.

In the emergency room before surgery, a dapper gentleman in a burgundy velveteen sport coat and hip glasses who looked like Elton John approached me calmly, syringe in hand. "I'll be your painkiller man," he said, and later when I remembered his introduction I thought it sounded like a great title for a rockin' blues song, but at that moment I knew his words would save me. I had never been so heartened to see any single human being in my life.

The surgery went well; there was now a titanium post in my leg, attached by screws at the ankle. I'd never broken anything before and the nurse reminded me that this was a compound whopper. She gave me a glass of water and two saltines. The physician assistant came in and said I would be in the hospital for at least a couple of days. The surgeon stopped by and announced that everything had gone well, that I should be up and walking in "Oh, I'd say about four or five months." The nurse appeared again and took my order for the following day's breakfast: oatmeal, blueberry pancakes, fresh fruit and eggs. She mentioned that the physical therapist would see me in the morning, with my choice of crutches or a walker.

It was all happening in a mist of modern-day pharmaceuticals. Everywhere I looked people were waiting on me. It was all I had wished for and more, yesterday in my bedroom, defeated by the dusty pile, lying on my ironic bed of self-pity.

Yet there was an undercurrent of worry, of panic even, that the fast-service drugs could not control. It was the Mother Undercurrent. There wasn't a blue uniformed employee on staff who could do anything about it, not with a fluff of the pillow or a shot in the arm.

★ ★ ★

Will had been laughing and playing at his friend Rina's house. Once upon a time she was an assistant in his kindergarten; now she was an education specialist with a doctorate. They'd stayed buddies the whole time, and even now that Will was in high school Rina would come every month to pick him up and take him to her house for an evening, to visit with her husband and their little daughter. It was his joy. He'd hang around the family's cozy home and play with their cat, Abby, or flip through Rina's photo books of kindergarten days. He felt safe enough to be perfectly social. But on this night in the midst of the party, Will's father called from the hospital. All the fun stopped.

"Mom has to stay in the hospital overnight," Will said to himself and to his dad over and over again in the car on the way home. "Mom has to stay in the hospital overnight." At age fifteen he'd matured in so many ways, but the last thousand-foot-high wall—oh, how I'd tried to chip away at it year after year—was separation from Mom. It brought on unbelievable anxiety, and now he, along with his poor father, looked out the car windshield into the scary night ahead without any of the usual preparation exercises.

Back in my hospital bed, I stared at Oprah Winfrey's head hanging high from the ceiling of my room. I switched off the TV sound with my remote, and as O went on mouthing her words, my worry over Will halted for a second as one precious, glorious, god-given thought swirled round my groggy brain. Will hadn't been there. When I hit the ground and there was a sound like a tree branch cracking and the bone stuck through my skin and I screamed bloody murder for five long minutes until the neighbors found me—Will wasn't there. For the sirens and the horrendous move to the gurney and the shakes and shivers of trauma, he was conveniently gone. He was often with me—he was always with me. Instead, while I wailed, Will had been with his friend, laughing away. Somebody up there liked me.

But that was the lovely gift Will and I had been given before the bomb dropped on our holiday season. By Thanksgiving, three things had happened to our family. I was an invalid, recovering from surgery, barely able to get from one place to another, teetering on the brink of depression, out of work with no sick pay (the life of a freelance artist and part-time teacher), and completely dependent on my miraculous husband and precious friends, plus an in-home nurse and a bath assistant, Miss Vicky, sent by our insurance company. Charles was reborn as saint and slave, doing everything for everybody, trapped in the crazy upheaval. And Will's militaristic routine, a schedule enforced by him and regularly obeyed by me, had been unexpectedly and completely blown out of the water.

It was enough for me to gaze at the calendar and try to fathom that, all the way from Christmas through to the buds of spring, I would be a girl with a handicap. But at least in my adult wisdom I knew I'd have to steel myself, and summon patience as never before. At least I knew, and knew so well and continued to remind everyone and myself, that this was far from a round of chemotherapy. But Will was about to go off his rocker. Mom drove him to school every day, faithfully stocked the house with his specific and limited foods, made all his meals (he required a particular size lettuce piece on his tuna sandwich), spoon-fed him his medication morning and night while cracking the same familiar joke, in the same funny voice, with the same rhythm and beat before the punch line. I followed up his meds with gummy bear vitamins—red ones only, never orange, never yellow; I took him to shoot hoops every Sunday but he didn't want to go to just one basketball court—he felt he needed to visit five different ones across the city. There were a thousand things I'd delivered blindly, some of which had come from a place of motherly love and had probably given Will the sense of security that contributed to his being such a happy boy. And I had to give myself credit for the fact that I had most certainly maneuvered many of his routines into non-existence after years of cajoling. But most of these rituals, which I'd innocently and laughingly bought into when they were seedlings, had shot up into scary, towering, massive redwoods I couldn't scale, no matter what grade of climbing equipment I dragged to the base of their trunks. "Mom, you are running around the house like chicken with head cut off!" was the line Will chirped in the morning, every morning. And lucky Will, for most of my chicken activity was in his service. Now Dad was doing the running, and plenty of it, and as the sun came up the fallen parent merely waited in the dark for someone to come and help her from the bed to the couch. Everything felt strange. Our family dynamic was brand new, and none of us, it seemed, would be able to get comfortable on this terribly bumpy ride.

At first Will tried all in the same breath to be nice to me, to exert control, and to fill the empty hole in his life. "The doctor says you'll be better in a week!" he hollered around the house over and over again. "By Monday you'll be walking! By Monday you'll be driving!" But as a couple of Mondays went by and I lay in the same place, he realized he was up against something huge. If I tried to explain the length of the healing process he simply could not grasp it; if I tried to show him how each day I got a little better (from walker to crutches!) he turned away. He got angry. He was, in many ways hidden and some ways plain, a teenager after all. By day he held on tight, knowing he could not let my catastrophe ruin his entire existence, but at night he lost his handle on things. "I'm taking this off!" he yelled one evening, after an hour of milder threats. He lunged at my cast. "Off!" He started to pull at it, and his exhausted father wrestled him away. Well, who could blame the boy for lashing out? He'd had to sacrifice almost everything that gave him a grip on life. He had to watch his mother, who had failed the crutches- on-steps test to the disappointment of her physical therapist, crawl up and down the stairs in our house every day on her hands and bottom, a lowly and pathetic creature if ever there was one. He was desperate. For a number of nights in a row, Will tried aggressively to get at the evil cast, and our living room erupted in scenes that left me in tears. Charles and I called this side of him "Dark Boy", and we were certain that under no circumstances could the patient be left alone with him. When my husband finally went back to work we'd have to get a sitter—for me.

There wouldn't be a problem finding extra security, should we need it. A spirited team of friends and neighbors were constantly offering themselves as helpers, appearing out of the blue to cook and clean and cheer me. I was humbled and grateful. But only a few close cohorts could know that the broken leg part, even with its mind-boggling disadvantages, was the no-big-deal part. Superwomen left savory casseroles in my kitchen and flew off down the street, and when they were gone the challenge of autism lay before me, looming larger than any wretched inconvenience.

★ ★ ★

December moved in with branch-whipping windstorms. I read something on my favorite new website, MyBrokenLeg.com—"Lower limb loss of any kind is usually accompanied by extreme psychological challenge." ("Yes," I nodded aloud to the computer screen)—so every day I woke up in bed and with my leg and other crutch-weary parts of my body as stiff as plywood, tried to find the good in my situation. There were ways. I hired a student of mine to do my Christmas shopping and mailing, and felt all-powerful. Charles took me out in the wheelchair and a smile lit up my whole face as I breathed in the cold pine-needle air of the outdoor world I was missing so much. On the coffee table by the couch where it seemed I'd already spent forever, a propped-up card sent by a friend matched the winter weather that blew at our door. It showed a black and white photo of a little girl standing on a rock, her arms flung out to the sky. Across the top it read: "We cannot direct the wind, but we can adjust our sails."

I tried to think positively. But I knew that inside my son's mind time was ticking and tension was building. With his therapist John, he was working with a visual timeline to help him understand how long this thing was going to drag on; he was going to receive prizes and rewards every week for his patience. The therapy seemed to be having a good effect. But one night in our living room as the Christmas tree lights twinkled away, Will left the calendar concept back in the therapist's office, and exploded: "I'm sick of this broken leg! I can't take it anymore!" He kicked his chair as he got up and moved toward me. Dark Boy was back.

"Will! Don't start in again," returned his father, standing up.

"I'm going to take off your boot! You are going to walk again tomorrow! You are going to walk like you did before!" His deep, loud, bellowing man's voice frightened me. It frightened me so much that, without wanting to, I screamed back at the same volume level.

"It won't be tomorrow, Will! It's going to be months. I've been trying to tell you! I know you don't want to hear it, but I'll be like this for months!"

He moved over to me and pushed hard on my bad leg, but his dad quickly grabbed him and pulled him off. I was shouting so loud I felt like I was losing all control.

"Will, get it through your head! I'm going to be like this for a long time!"

The sound startled him. His father let go of his shoulders and he wobbled backwards toward his chair. He sat down. I put my head in my hands, immediately regretting my outburst, but finally the room was silent. Our lovely tree kept on twinkling.

"I want you to walk, like normal, in a few days," he whimpered in a voice that was boyish now, and barely audible. It held a note of something I couldn't quite construe—defeat, or maybe even relief.

★ ★ ★

Christmas was everything to Will, and I wondered whether he would let a mini-tragedy override his favorite celebration. The bustle of the season had once put him on sensory overload, but recently his carol had changed its tune: now each year he became giddy with enchantment, soaring like a reindeer over everyone else's stress. He was in love with holidays in general, right down to President's Day and Martin Luther King's birthday. But he was all over Christmas like a cheap Santa suit.

And since our big blowout, something remarkable had occurred. He was quiet about the leg. He'd said nothing. Except once, going to bed, he looked at me out of the corner of his eye. "I hope you are feeling better," he said.

I was feeling better, in some ways. I was feeling better that Charles and I hadn't had any more experiences with Dark Boy. I was feeling like this was my time to lay and look out the window for hours at the bare branches of our maple trees, re-imagining what my life could be like when I got up again.

One day I saw Will get his own crackers out of the cupboard and put them on a plate. It was a first. "I get my own snacks now," he said. I noticed while crutch-hopping through the kitchen that the gummy bear vitamins were disappearing—even the orange and yellow ones. "I just give him all the colors whether he wants them or not," said my husband casually.

During one of my sofa reveries I thought back to an Autism Society summer picnic that Will and I had once attended when he was little. We sat on a bench in the sun next to a teenage boy and his mom. The boy didn't want to eat and shoved his plate of food into his mother's lap to make his point. "They turn into fascists," she told me, wiping mustard from her skirt. "Watch out."

And the mothers, innocent as lambs, turn into fascist-nurturers, I thought now.

By Christmas Eve day, Dark Boy had morphed into a cherub, even making all the beds in the house, another first. He chattered away about how fun it was going to be to open his presents. He hummed Christmas songs. A peaceful, clear morning was coming up. That was the day I noticed him writing in his journal—again.

He'd been keeping the diary for a year or so, scribbling in it every so often. But since I'd landed on the couch I'd witnessed more of this activity. Almost every day he sat at the dining room table where I had a great view of him, as he carefully printed a sentence, then tapped the pen on his chin as he stared out the window, letting the next line come. Like an actor, playing an author.

This was the way his mother coped with anything that came down the pike—with journal at the ready and pen in hand, furiously scribbling emotionally charged, run-on sentences to which no editor would dare or have the right to take a colored pen. In fact I'd been using this method a lot of late, when I felt trapped, isolated, barred completely from all the great fun and action of life. Was my son following in my self-help footsteps? I couldn't wait for Will to close the book and go downstairs to play video games—since he always proudly insisted I read his entries, I knew there was no problem in my taking a peek. He disappeared from the room. I put on my reading glasses, rose up on my crutches and floated over to the table with surprising ease, so geared up was I to read, in the words of my favorite writer, the story of my terrible fate.

November 28th
Today I stayed home from school because there was snow. I really liked the snow! The snow was white. I saw some kids sledding! I threw snowballs with my dad!

December 1st
In first period I always work in the school library. I filed books in the library today and pushed in chairs. I don't have to go to school tomorrow because it is Saturday!

I adjusted my glasses to a different place on my nose. What was this? No mention of the fact that his entire world had turned upside down? Not a word about what it was like to have his religious routine torn to remnants overnight? Disappointment hovered over me, but I read on. I soon understood what all those exclamation points were pointing to.

December 6th
In school today I went shopping at the grocery store! It was fun! I bought bread, crackers, and peanut butter. I looked at fruits and vegetables too!

Denial, the unhealthy but time-honored mechanism. Avoidance, resistance—the prevailing hallmarks of Will's personality type. During this challenging and miserable time of his family's life, he was trying to make believe it wasn't happening. Not only that. Will was a fifteen-year-old kid and he was used to having control. He wanted normal, and he'd find a way to get it.

December 24th
We are going to have a really fun Christmas. I always go to my Grandma's house for Christmas Day. This will be my best Christmas ever!

I closed the diary with my exclamation point meter on tilt, but a sense of calm came over me. The guy was using the best parts of the story of his life to get himself through this anxious time. Well, more power to him, I thought; we all have our ways, and I'd been the mother, as a matter of fact, who constantly reminded him that one must focus on the good and wonderful parts of one's life. Something occurred to me: when this whole thing was over, Will and his father and I could sit down together to try to confront reality in hindsight. We'd have a family talk about what we all went through. About what we all learned. Will was good at that, at seeing things clearly once the chaos was past.

And so Christmas came and went, and Will said it was his best Christmas ever.

At the end of December the doc told me I would be walking—with the help of my crutches, and doubtless with some initial pain but, by God, walking!—by the end of January, weeks sooner than anyone had expected. The bone was healing fast, strong and straight; I would even be able to drive, privilege of privileges. My wheelchair man, Charles, rolled me out of the appointment into a crystal blue afternoon, each of us as ebullient as on our wedding day. There was light at the end of the crazy tunnel. What had happened to me? I had been given my wish (be careful what you wish for). I had asked, and I had received. Now I would rise again, with a new skip in my step. Everything that seemed like an obligation before the accident now looked like an opportunity. Things I didn't feel I had the power to change when the sky was the color of slate, I knew now, as the New Year shed a little golden sun, I could change. I would change.

And my teenage boy, who made the beds, who prepared his own snack, who wrote stories in a journal to try to make sense of life, did finally get a prize for his patience, a token to make up for his pain. He learned that he couldn't direct the wind, as I had accidentally led him to believe he could. But he caught something on the breeze: the notion that, in spite of whatever storms nature would surely put him through, he might one day be a master, a captain in total command, of adjusting his sails.

February 2nd—Groundhog Day!
Today is a holiday called Groundhog Day! My mom's leg is better and she drove
me to school. Today I did money math. I did my yoga class. School was fun!

About the Author

Kelly Harland is a Seattle vocalist, writer and voice teacher. She is on the faculty of the music department at Cornish College of the Arts, and as a singer is currently working on her third CD of jazz standards. Her credits include television and radio commercials, vocal work on many CDs, and performances in clubs and concerts. She has written articles for the magazine Autism Advocate and contributed to the Cup of Comfort book series. At home in Seattle she enjoys being with Will and her husband Chuck Deardorf, a college music professor who also maintains an illustrious career as a jazz bassist. They have a mischievous cat named Georgie. In summer the family loves to travel by ferryboat into the San Juan Islands north of Seattle for peace and glorious views, and each August they journey to Vancouver BC for city fun.